MznLnx

Missing Links Exam Preps

Exam Prep for

Urban Economics

O'Sullivan, 6th Edition

The MznLnx Exam Prep is your link from the texbook and lecture to your exams.
The MznLnx Exam Preps are unauthorized and comprehensive reviews of your textbooks.

All material provided by MznLnx and Rico Publications (c) 2010
Textbook publishers and textbook authors do not particpate in or contribute to these reviews.

MznLnx

Rico
Publications

Exam Prep for Urban Economics
6th Edition
O'Sullivan

Publisher: Raymond Houge
Assistant Editor: Michael Rouger
Text and Cover Designer: Lisa Buckner
Marketing Manager: Sara Swagger
Project Manager, Editorial Production: Jerry Emerson
Art Director: Vernon Lowerui

Product Manager: Dave Mason
Editorial Assitant: Rachel Guzmanji
Pedagogy: Debra Long
Cover Image: Jim Reed/Getty Images
Text and Cover Printer: City Printing, Inc.
Compositor: Media Mix, Inc.

(c) 2010 Rico Publications

ALL RIGHTS RESERVED. No part of this work covered by the copyright may be reproduced or used in any form or by an means--graphic, electronic, or mechanical, including photocopying, recording, taping, Web distribution, information storage, and retrieval systems, or in any other manner--without the written permission of the publisher.

Printed in the United States
ISBN:

For more information about our products, contact us at:
Dave.Mason@RicoPublications.com

For permission to use material from this text or product, submit a request online to:
Dave.Mason@RicoPublications.com

Contents

CHAPTER 1
Introduction and Axioms of Urban Economics — 1

CHAPTER 2
Why Do Cities Exist? — 6

CHAPTER 3
Why Do Firms Cluster? — 13

CHAPTER 4
City Size — 18

CHAPTER 5
Urban Growth — 22

CHAPTER 6
Urban Land Rent — 31

CHAPTER 7
Land-Use Patternsr — 38

CHAPTER 8
Neighborhood Choice — 48

CHAPTER 9
Zoning and Growth Controls — 61

CHAPTER 10
Externalities from Autos — 72

CHAPTER 11
Mass Transit — 79

CHAPTER 12
Crime — 87

CHAPTER 13
Why Is Housing Different? — 91

CHAPTER 14
Housing Policy — 95

CHAPTER 15
The Role of Local Government — 104

CHAPTER 16
Local Government Revenue — 114

ANSWER KEY — 127

TO THE STUDENT

COMPREHENSIVE

The *MznLnx* Exam Prep series is designed to help you pass your exams. Editors at MznLnx review your textbooks and then prepare these practice exams to help you master the textbook material. Unlike study guides, workbooks, and practice tests provided by the texbook publisher and textbook authors, *MznLnx* gives you **all** of the material in each chapter in exam form, not just samples, so you can be sure to nail your exam.

MECHANICAL

The MznLnx Exam Prep series creates exams that will help you learn the subject matter as well as test you on your understanding. Each question is designed to help you master the concept. Just working through the exams, you gain an understanding of the subject--its a simple mechanical process that produces success.

INTEGRATED STUDY GUIDE AND REVIEW

MznLnx is not just a set of exams designed to test you, its also a comprehensive review of the subject content. Each exam question is also a review of the concept, making sure that you will get the answer correct without having to go to other sources of material. You learn as you go! Its the easiest way to pass an exam.

HUMOR

Studying can be tedious and dry. MznLnx's instructional design includes moderate humor within the exam questions on occassion, to break the tedium and revitalize the brain

Chapter 1. Introduction and Axioms of Urban Economics

1. _____ is broadly the economic study of urban areas. As such, it involves using the tools of economics to analyze urban issues such as crime, education, public transit, housing, and local government finance. More narrowly, it is a branch of microeconomics that studies urban spatial structure and the location of households and firms.
    a. Urban economics
    b. ACCRA Cost of Living Index
    c. AD-IA Model
    d. ACEA agreement

2. _____s is the social science that studies the production, distribution, and consumption of goods and services. The term _____s comes from the Ancient Greek oá¼°κονομῖα from oá¼¶κος (oikos, 'house') + vÏŒμος (nomos, 'custom' or 'law'), hence 'rules of the house(hold)'. Current _____ models developed out of the broader field of political economy in the late 19th century, owing to a desire to use an empirical approach more akin to the physical sciences.
    a. Opportunity cost
    b. Inflation
    c. Energy economics
    d. Economic

3. A _____ is the procedure of systematically acquiring and recording information about the members of a given population. It is a regularly occurring and official count of a particular population. The term is used mostly in connection with national 'population and door to door _____es' (to be taken every 10 years according to United Nations recommendations), agriculture, and business _____es.
    a. Census
    b. 1921 recession
    c. 130-30 fund
    d. 100-year flood

4. In microeconomics, _____ is quite simply the conversion of inputs into outputs. It is an economic process that uses resources to create a good or service that is suitable for exchange. This can include manufacturing, storing, shipping, and packaging.
    a. MET
    b. Red Guards
    c. Solved
    d. Production

5. In the study of human settlements, an _____ is an extended city or town area comprising the built-up area of a central place (usually a municipality) and any suburbs linked by continuous urban area. In France, INSEE the French Statistical Institute, translate it as 'Unité urbaine' which means continuous urbanized area. However, because of differences in definitions of what does and does not constitute an '_____', as well as variations and limitations in statistical or geographical methodology, it can be problematic to compare different _____s around the world.

Chapter 1. Introduction and Axioms of Urban Economics

a. ACCRA Cost of Living Index
b. ACEA agreement
c. AD-IA Model
d. Agglomeration

6. _____ is a set of properties and characteristics of the environment, either generalized or local, as they impinge on human beings and other organisms.

_____ is a general term which can refer to varied characteristics that relate to the natural environment as well as the built environment, such as air and water purity or pollution, noise and the potential effects which such characteristics may have on physical and mental health caused by human activities.

In the USA the term is applied with a body of federal and state standards and regulations that are monitored by regulatory agencies.

a. Environmental quality
b. ACEA agreement
c. AD-IA Model
d. ACCRA Cost of Living Index

7. _____ is the physical growth of rural or natural land into urban areas as a result of population immigration to an existing urban area. Effects include change in density and administration services. While the exact definition and population size of urbanized areas varies among different countries, _____ is attributed to growth of cities.

a. Urban renewal
b. ACCRA Cost of Living Index
c. Urban prairie
d. Urbanization

8. _____ in economics and business is the result of an exchange and from that trade we assign a numerical monetary value to a good, service or asset. If Alice trades Bob 4 apples for an orange, the _____ of an orange is 4 apples. Inversely, the _____ of an apple is 1/4 oranges.

a. Price war
b. Premium pricing
c. Price
d. Price book

9. _____ is the increase in the amount of the goods and services produced by an economy over time. It is conventionally measured as the percent rate of increase in real gross domestic product, or real GDP. Growth is usually calculated in real terms, i.e. inflation-adjusted terms, in order to net out the effect of inflation on the price of the goods and services produced.
   a. ACCRA Cost of Living Index
   b. AD-IA Model
   c. Economic growth
   d. ACEA agreement

10. The term '_____' refers to the concept of collecting information and attempting to spot a pattern in the information. In some fields of study, the term '_____' has more formally-defined meanings.

In project management _____ is a mathematical technique that uses historical results to predict future outcome.

   a. Coefficient of determination
   b. Probit model
   c. Trend analysis
   d. Quantile regression

11. _____ is a mechanism that allows people easily to buy and sell products. Services are often included in the scope of the term. _____ regulation is an economic term that describes restrictions in the market.
   a. Fixed exchange rate system
   b. Product market
   c. Market dominance
   d. Financialization

12. Necessary _____s:

If x is a necessary _____ of y, then the presence of y necessarily implies the presence of x. The presence of x, however, does not imply that y will occur.

Sufficient _____s:

If x is a sufficient _____ of y, then the presence of x necessarily implies the presence of y.

Chapter 1. Introduction and Axioms of Urban Economics

a. Philosophy of economics
b. Materialism
c. Political philosophy
d. Cause

13. _____, in microeconomics, are the cost advantages that a business obtains due to expansion. They are factors that cause a producere;s average cost per unit to fall as scale is increased. _____ is a long run concept and refers to reductions in unit cost as the size of a facility, or scale, increases.

   a. Economies of scale
   b. Underinvestment employment relationship
   c. Isoquant
   d. Economic production quantity

14. _____ is the term denoting either an entrance or changes which are inserted into a system and which activate/modify a process. It is an abstract concept, used in the modeling, system(s) design and system(s) exploitation. It is usually connected with other terms, e.g., _____ field, _____ variable, _____ parameter, _____ value, _____ signal, _____ device and _____ file.

   a. ACEA agreement
   b. Input
   c. AD-IA Model
   d. ACCRA Cost of Living Index

15. In economics, _____ is the difference between a company's total revenue and its opportunity costs. It is the increase in wealth that an investor has from making an investment, taking into consideration all costs associated with that investment including the opportunity cost of capital.

Profit is the factor income of the entrepreneur.

   a. Operating profit
   b. ACCRA Cost of Living Index
   c. Accounting profit
   d. Economic profit

16. _____ or economic opportunity loss is the value of the next best alternative foregone as the result of making a decision. _____ analysis is an important part of a company's decision-making processes but is not treated as an actual cost in any financial statement. The next best thing that a person can engage in is referred to as the _____ of doing the best thing and ignoring the next best thing to be done.

a. Opportunity cost
b. Industrial organization
c. Economic
d. Economic ideology

17. A _____ is the smallest geographic unit used by the United States Census Bureau for tabulation of 100-percent data (data collected from all houses, rather than a sample of houses.) Several blocks make up block groups, which again make up census tracts. There are on average about 39 blocks per block group, but there are variations.
a. 100-year flood
b. Census block
c. 1921 recession
d. 130-30 fund

18. A _____ is the official term for a functional region based around an urban center of at least 10,000 people, based on standards published by the Office of Management and Budget (OMB) in 2000. Areas defined on the basis of these standards applied with Census 2000 data were announced by OMB in June 2003. These standards are used to replace the definitions of metropolitan areas that were defined in 1990.
a. Core based statistical area
b. 1921 recession
c. 100-year flood
d. 130-30 fund

19. To _____ is to impose a financial charge or other levy upon a taxpayer by a state or the functional equivalent of a state.

_____es are also imposed by many subnational entities. _____es consist of direct _____ or indirect _____, and may be paid in money or as its labour equivalent (often but not always unpaid.)

a. Tax
b. 130-30 fund
c. 1921 recession
d. 100-year flood

Chapter 2. Why Do Cities Exist?

1. _____ was a survey conducted by the U.S. Department of Justice to gauge the prevalence of alcohol and illegal drug use among prior arrestees. It was a reformulation of the prior Drug Use Forecasting (DUF) program, focused on five drugs in particular: cocaine, marijuana, methamphetamine, opiates, and PCP.

Participants were randomly selected from arrest records in major metropolitan areas; because no personally identifying information is taken from each record chosen, the resulting data can be correlated to arrest rates, but not to the total population of persons charged.

   a. Arrestee Drug Abuse Monitoring
   b. ACCRA Cost of Living Index
   c. ACEA agreement
   d. AD-IA Model

2. In production, returns to scale refers to changes in output subsequent to a proportional change in all inputs (where all inputs increase by a constant factor.) If output increases by that same proportional change then there are _____ If output increases by less than that proportional change, there are decreasing returns to scale (DRS.)
   a. Long term
   b. Lexicographic preferences
   c. Consumer sovereignty
   d. Constant returns to scale

3. _____ was a Scottish moral philosopher and a pioneer of political economy. One of the key figures of the Scottish Enlightenment, Smith is the author of The Theory of Moral Sentiments and An Inquiry into the Nature and Causes of the Wealth of Nations. The latter, usually abbreviated as The Wealth of Nations, is considered his magnum opus and the first modern work of economics.
   a. Adolph Fischer
   b. Adam Smith
   c. Adolf Hitler
   d. Alan Greenspan

4. In microeconomics, _____ is quite simply the conversion of inputs into outputs. It is an economic process that uses resources to create a good or service that is suitable for exchange. This can include manufacturing, storing, shipping, and packaging.
   a. Red Guards
   b. Solved
   c. MET
   d. Production

5. _____ in economics refers to metrics and measures of output from production processes, per unit of input. Labor _____, for example, is typically measured as a ratio of output per labor-hour, an input. _____ may be conceived of as a metrics of the technical or engineering efficiency of production.
   a. Piece work
   b. Production-possibility frontier
   c. Fordism
   d. Productivity

6. In economics, _____ and economies of scale are related terms that describe what happens as the scale of production increases. They are different terms and should not be used interchangeably.

   _____ refers to a technical property of production that examines changes in output subsequent to a proportional change in all inputs (where all inputs increase by a constant factor.)

   a. Customer equity
   b. Constant returns to scale
   c. Necessity good
   d. Returns to scale

7. In economics, _____ refers to the ability of a person or a country to produce a particular good at a lower marginal cost and opportunity cost than another person or country. It is the ability to produce a product most efficiently given all the other products that could be produced. It can be contrasted with absolute advantage which refers to the ability of a person or a country to produce a particular good at a lower absolute cost than another.
   a. Triffin dilemma
   b. Hot money
   c. Gravity model of trade
   d. Comparative advantage

8. _____ in economics and business is the result of an exchange and from that trade we assign a numerical monetary value to a good, service or asset. If Alice trades Bob 4 apples for an orange, the _____ of an orange is 4 apples. Inversely, the _____ of an apple is 1/4 oranges.
   a. Premium pricing
   b. Price war
   c. Price book
   d. Price

9. _____, in microeconomics, are the cost advantages that a business obtains due to expansion. They are factors that cause a producere;s average cost per unit to fall as scale is increased. _____ is a long run concept and refers to reductions in unit cost as the size of a facility, or scale, increases.
   a. Underinvestment employment relationship
   b. Economies of scale
   c. Isoquant
   d. Economic production quantity

10. In economics and related disciplines, a _____ is a cost incurred in making an economic exchange. For example, most people, when buying or selling a stock, must pay a commission to their broker; that commission is a _____ of doing the stock deal. Or consider buying a banana from a store; to purchase the banana, your costs will be not only the price of the banana itself, but also the energy and effort it requires to find out which of the various banana products you prefer, where to get them and at what price, the cost of traveling from your house to the store and back, the time waiting in line, and the effort of the paying itself; the costs above and beyond the cost of the banana are the _____s.
   a. Transaction cost
   b. Sliding scale fees
   c. Cost of poor quality
   d. Cost allocation

11. In the study of human settlements, an _____ is an extended city or town area comprising the built-up area of a central place (usually a municipality) and any suburbs linked by continuous urban area. In France, INSEE the French Statistical Institute, translate it as 'Unité urbaine' which means continuous urbanized area. However, because of differences in definitions of what does and does not constitute an '_____', as well as variations and limitations in statistical or geographical methodology, it can be problematic to compare different _____s around the world.
   a. ACEA agreement
   b. Agglomeration
   c. AD-IA Model
   d. ACCRA Cost of Living Index

12. Network externalities resemble economies of scale, but they are not considered such because they are a function of the number of users of a good or service in an industry, not of the production efficiency within a business. _____ are only considered examples of network externalities if they are driven by demand side economies.

Formally, a production function $F(K, L)$ is defined to have:

- constant returns to scale if (for any constant a greater than or equal to 0) $F(aK, aL) = aF(K, L)$
- increasing returns to scale if (for any constant a greater than 1) $F(aK, aL) > aF(K, L)$,
- decreasing returns to scale if (for any constant a greater than 1) $F(aK, aL) < aF(K, L)$

where K and L are factors of production, capital and labour, respectively.

As an example, the Cobb-Douglas functional form has constant returns to scale when the sum of the exponents adds up to one.

a. ACEA agreement
b. AD-IA Model
c. ACCRA Cost of Living Index
d. Economies of scale external to the firm

13. A _____ is an independent country whose territory consists solely of a single major city and the area immediately surrounding it. The term '_____' should not be confused with 'independent city', which refers to a city which is not administered as part of another local government.

Whereas the nation-states rely on a common cultural heritage, be it linguistic, historical, religious, economic, etc., the _____ relies on the common interest in the function of the urban center.

a. City-state
b. 1921 recession
c. 100-year flood
d. 130-30 fund

14. A polis -- plural: poleis -- is a city, a city-state and also citizenship and body of citizens. When used to describe Classical Athens and its contemporaries, polis is often translated as 'city-state.'

The word originates from the ancient _____, which developed during the Archaic period, the ancestor of city, state and citizenship, and persisted (though with decreasing influence) well into Roman times, when the equivalent Latin word was civitas, also meaning 'citizenhood', while municipium applied to a non-sovereign local entity. The term city-state which originated in English does not fully translate the Greek term.

a. 130-30 fund
b. 100-year flood
c. 1921 recession
d. Greek city-states

15. The _____ Tiebout migration is a public choice theory model first described by economist Charles Tiebout in his article 'A Pure Theory of Local Expenditures' The essence of the model is that there is in fact a non-political solution to the free rider problem in local governance.

Tiebout first proposed the model informally as a graduate student in a seminar with Richard Musgrave, who argued that the free rider problem necessarily required a political solution.

a. Tiebout model
b. 130-30 fund
c. 100-year flood
d. 1921 recession

16. The _____ was a period in the late 18th and early 19th centuries when major changes in agriculture, manufacturing, mining, and transportation had a profound effect on the socioeconomic and cultural conditions in Britain. The changes subsequently spread throughout Europe, North America, and eventually the world. The onset of the _____ marked a major turning point in human society; almost every aspect of daily life was eventually influenced in some way.
a. Industrial Revolution
b. Adolf Hitler
c. Adam Smith
d. Adolph Fischer

17. _____ was an American inventor best known as the inventor of the cotton gin. This was one of the key inventions of the industrial revolution and shaped the economy of the antebellum South. Whitney's invention made short staple cotton into a profitable crop, which strengthened the economic foundation of slavery.
a. Oskar Morgenstern
b. Andrew Carnegie
c. Alfred Marshall
d. Eli Whitney

18. A _____ is a geographic zone containing the people who are likely to purchase a firm's goods or services.
a. 100-year flood
b. Market area
c. Decommercialization
d. Sugging

19. The _____ involves semi-skilled labor using machine tools and templates (or jigs) to make standardized, identical, interchangeable parts, manufactured to a tolerance. The system is also known as the armory practice because of the history of its development by the United States Department of War in the Springfield and Harpers Ferry armories.

Since parts are interchangeable, it is also possible to separate manufacture from assembly, and assembly may be carried out by semi-skilled labor on an assembly line - an example of the division of labor.

a. ACEA agreement
b. ACCRA Cost of Living Index
c. American System of Manufacturing
d. AD-IA Model

20. _____ is the production of large amounts of standardized products, including and especially on assembly lines. The concepts of _____ are applied to various kinds of products, from fluids and particulates handled in bulk to discrete solid parts to assemblies of such parts

_____ of assemblies typically uses electric-motor-powered moving tracks or conveyor belts to move partially complete products to workers, who perform simple repetitive tasks.

a. 100-year flood
b. Mass production
c. 1921 recession
d. 130-30 fund

21. _____s are a type of administrative division, in some countries managed by a local government. They vary greatly in size, spanning entire regions or counties, several municipalities, or subdivisions of municipalities.

In Austria, a _____ or Bezirk is an administrative division normally encompassing several municipalities, roughly equivalent to the Landkreis in Germany.

a. 130-30 fund
b. 100-year flood
c. 1921 recession
d. District

22. _____ is a set of properties and characteristics of the environment, either generalized or local, as they impinge on human beings and other organisms.

_____ is a general term which can refer to varied characteristics that relate to the natural environment as well as the built environment, such as air and water purity or pollution, noise and the potential effects which such characteristics may have on physical and mental health caused by human activities.

In the USA the term is applied with a body of federal and state standards and regulations that are monitored by regulatory agencies.

Chapter 2. Why Do Cities Exist?

a. Environmental quality
b. ACCRA Cost of Living Index
c. ACEA agreement
d. AD-IA Model

23. _____s is the social science that studies the production, distribution, and consumption of goods and services. The term _____s comes from the Ancient Greek oá¼°κονομῖα from oá¼¶κος (oikos, 'house') + vÏŒμος (nomos, 'custom' or 'law'), hence 'rules of the house(hold)'. Current _____ models developed out of the broader field of political economy in the late 19th century, owing to a desire to use an empirical approach more akin to the physical sciences.
    a. Inflation
    b. Energy economics
    c. Economic
    d. Opportunity cost

24. In economics, _____ is the difference between a company's total revenue and its opportunity costs. It is the increase in wealth that an investor has from making an investment, taking into consideration all costs associated with that investment including the opportunity cost of capital.

Profit is the factor income of the entrepreneur.

    a. ACCRA Cost of Living Index
    b. Economic profit
    c. Accounting profit
    d. Operating profit

25. _____ is a mechanism that allows people easily to buy and sell products. Services are often included in the scope of the term. _____ regulation is an economic term that describes restrictions in the market.
    a. Product market
    b. Fixed exchange rate system
    c. Financialization
    d. Market dominance

Chapter 3. Why Do Firms Cluster?

1. In the study of human settlements, an _____ is an extended city or town area comprising the built-up area of a central place (usually a municipality) and any suburbs linked by continuous urban area. In France, INSEE the French Statistical Institute, translate it as 'Unité urbaine' which means continuous urbanized area. However, because of differences in definitions of what does and does not constitute an '_____', as well as variations and limitations in statistical or geographical methodology, it can be problematic to compare different _____s around the world.
    a. AD-IA Model
    b. ACEA agreement
    c. ACCRA Cost of Living Index
    d. Agglomeration

2. _____s is the social science that studies the production, distribution, and consumption of goods and services. The term _____s comes from the Ancient Greek οἰκονομία from οἶκος (oikos, 'house') + νόμος (nomos, 'custom' or 'law'), hence 'rules of the house(hold)'. Current _____ models developed out of the broader field of political economy in the late 19th century, owing to a desire to use an empirical approach more akin to the physical sciences.
    a. Inflation
    b. Opportunity cost
    c. Energy economics
    d. Economic

3. _____ is the increase in the amount of the goods and services produced by an economy over time. It is conventionally measured as the percent rate of increase in real gross domestic product, or real GDP. Growth is usually calculated in real terms, i.e. inflation-adjusted terms, in order to net out the effect of inflation on the price of the goods and services produced.
    a. Economic growth
    b. ACCRA Cost of Living Index
    c. AD-IA Model
    d. ACEA agreement

4. _____ is the physical growth of rural or natural land into urban areas as a result of population immigration to an existing urban area. Effects include change in density and administration services. While the exact definition and population size of urbanized areas varies among different countries, _____ is attributed to growth of cities.
    a. Urban prairie
    b. Urbanization
    c. ACCRA Cost of Living Index
    d. Urban renewal

Chapter 3. Why Do Firms Cluster?

5. _____ is the term denoting either an entrance or changes which are inserted into a system and which activate/modify a process. It is an abstract concept, used in the modeling, system(s) design and system(s) exploitation. It is usually connected with other terms, e.g., _____ field, _____ variable, _____ parameter, _____ value, _____ signal, _____ device and _____ file.
   a. AD-IA Model
   b. ACEA agreement
   c. Input
   d. ACCRA Cost of Living Index

6. In microeconomics, _____ is quite simply the conversion of inputs into outputs. It is an economic process that uses resources to create a good or service that is suitable for exchange. This can include manufacturing, storing, shipping, and packaging.
   a. MET
   b. Production
   c. Solved
   d. Red Guards

7. _____, in microeconomics, are the cost advantages that a business obtains due to expansion. They are factors that cause a producere;s average cost per unit to fall as scale is increased. _____ is a long run concept and refers to reductions in unit cost as the size of a facility, or scale, increases.
   a. Isoquant
   b. Underinvestment employment relationship
   c. Economic production quantity
   d. Economies of scale

8. _____ in economics and business is the result of an exchange and from that trade we assign a numerical monetary value to a good, service or asset. If Alice trades Bob 4 apples for an orange, the _____ of an orange is 4 apples. Inversely, the _____ of an apple is 1/4 oranges.
   a. Price book
   b. Price war
   c. Premium pricing
   d. Price

9. _____ refers to the stock of skills and knowledge embodied in the ability to perform labor so as to produce economic value. It is the skills and knowledge gained by a worker through education and experience.Many early economic theories refer to it simply as labor, one of three factors of production, and consider it to be a fungible resource -- homogeneous and easily interchangeable. Other conceptions of labor dispense with these assumptions.

a. Law of increasing costs
b. General equilibrium
c. Price theory
d. Human capital

10. In microeconomics, _____ is the extra revenue that an additional unit of product will bring. It is the additional income from selling one more unit of a good; sometimes equal to price. It can also be described as the change in total revenue/change in number of units sold.

a. Long term
b. Marginal revenue
c. Reservation price
d. Market demand schedule

11. The marginal revenue productivity theory of wages, also referred to as the _____ of labor, is the change in total revenue earned by a firm that results from employing one more unit of labor. It is a neoclassical model that determines, under some conditions, the optimal number of workers to employ at an exogenously determined market wage rate.

The _____ of a worker is equal to the product of the marginal product of labor (MP) and the marginal revenue (MR), given by MR×MP = _____.

a. Marginal revenue productivity theory of wages
b. Real prices and ideal prices
c. Coal depletion
d. Marginal revenue product

12. A _____ is a set of exclusive rights granted by a state to an inventor or his assignee for a limited period of time in exchange for a disclosure of an invention.

The procedure for granting _____s, the requirements placed on the _____ee and the extent of the exclusive rights vary widely between countries according to national laws and international agreements. Typically, however, a _____ application must include one or more claims defining the invention which must be new, inventive, and useful or industrially applicable.

a. Patent
b. Bank regulation
c. Long service leave
d. Bona fide occupational qualification

Chapter 3. Why Do Firms Cluster?

13. Network externalities resemble economies of scale, but they are not considered such because they are a function of the number of users of a good or service in an industry, not of the production efficiency within a business. _____ are only considered examples of network externalities if they are driven by demand side economies.

Formally, a production function $F(K, L)$ is defined to have:

- constant returns to scale if (for any constant a greater than or equal to 0) $F(aK, aL) = aF(K, L)$
- increasing returns to scale if (for any constant a greater than 1) $F(aK, aL) > aF(K, L)$,
- decreasing returns to scale if (for any constant a greater than 1) $F(aK, aL) < aF(K, L)$

where K and L are factors of production, capital and labour, respectively.

As an example, the Cobb-Douglas functional form has constant returns to scale when the sum of the exponents adds up to one.

a. Economies of scale external to the firm
b. ACCRA Cost of Living Index
c. ACEA agreement
d. AD-IA Model

14. The _____ is 'the basic residential unit in which economic production, consumption, inheritance, child rearing, and shelter are organized and carried out'; [the _____] 'may or may not be synonomous with family'.

The _____ is the basic unit of analysis in many social, microeconomic and government models. The term refers to all individuals who live in the same dwelling.

a. Family economics
b. Household
c. 130-30 fund
d. 100-year flood

15. The supply of labor is the number of total hours that workers wish to work at a given real wage rate.

_____ curves are derived from the 'labor-leisure' trade-off. More hours worked earn higher incomes but necessitate a cut in the amount of leisure that workers enjoy.

a. Labor supply
b. Late capitalism
c. Human trafficking
d. Creative capitalism

Chapter 4. City Size

1. In the study of human settlements, an _____ is an extended city or town area comprising the built-up area of a central place (usually a municipality) and any suburbs linked by continuous urban area. In France, INSEE the French Statistical Institute, translate it as 'Unité urbaine' which means continuous urbanized area. However, because of differences in definitions of what does and does not constitute an '_____', as well as variations and limitations in statistical or geographical methodology, it can be problematic to compare different _____s around the world.
    a. ACCRA Cost of Living Index
    b. AD-IA Model
    c. ACEA agreement
    d. Agglomeration

2. In economics, _____ is a measure of the relative satisfaction from consumption of various goods and services. Given this measure, one may speak meaningfully of increasing or decreasing _____, and thereby explain economic behavior in terms of attempts to increase one's _____. For illustrative purposes, changes in _____ are sometimes expressed in units called utils.
    a. Ordinal utility
    b. Utility
    c. Utility function
    d. Expected utility hypothesis

3. _____ in economics and business is the result of an exchange and from that trade we assign a numerical monetary value to a good, service or asset. If Alice trades Bob 4 apples for an orange, the _____ of an orange is 4 apples. Inversely, the _____ of an apple is 1/4 oranges.
    a. Price
    b. Price book
    c. Premium pricing
    d. Price war

4. Economic _____ is defined as an excess distribution to any factor in a production process above that which is required to induce the factor into the process or any excess above that which is necessary to keep the factor in its current use..

Classical Factor _____ is primarily concerned with the fee paid for the use of fixed (e.g. natural) resources. The classical definition is expressed as any excess payment above that required to induce or provide for production.

   a. 1921 recession
   b. 130-30 fund
   c. 100-year flood
   d. Rent

Chapter 4. City Size

5. A _____ is a situation that involves losing one quality or aspect of something in return for gaining another quality or aspect. It implies a decision to be made with full comprehension of both the upside and downside of a particular choice.

In economics the term is expressed as opportunity cost, referring the most preferred alternative given up.

   a. Whitemail
   b. Trade-off
   c. Nonmarket
   d. Friedman-Savage utility function

6. A _____ is an object whose consumption increases the utility of the consumer, for which the quantity demanded exceeds the quantity supplied at zero price. _____s are usually modeled as having diminishing marginal utility. The first individual purchase has high utility; the second has less.
   a. Merit good
   b. Composite good
   c. Pie method
   d. Good

7. _____ is the physical growth of rural or natural land into urban areas as a result of population immigration to an existing urban area. Effects include change in density and administration services. While the exact definition and population size of urbanized areas varies among different countries, _____ is attributed to growth of cities.
   a. Urban renewal
   b. Urban prairie
   c. ACCRA Cost of Living Index
   d. Urbanization

8. A _____ is:

- Rewrite _____, in generative grammar and computer science
- Standardization, a formal and widely-accepted statement, fact, definition, or qualification
- Operation, a determinate _____ for performing a mathematical operation and obtaining a certain result (Mathematics, Logic)
    - Unary operation
    - Binary operation
- _____ of inference, a function from sets of formulae to formulae (Mathematics, Logic)
- _____ of thumb, principle with broad application that is not intended to be strictly accurate or reliable for every situation. Also often simply referred to as a _____
- Moral, an atomic element of a moral code for guiding choices in human behavior
- Heuristic, a quantized '_____' which shows a tendency or probability for successful function
- A regulation, as in sports
- A Production _____, as in computer science
- Procedural law, a _____ set governing the application of laws to cases
    - A law, which may informally be called a '_____'
    - A court ruling, a decision by a court
- In the U.S. Government, a regulation mandated by Congress, but written or expanded upon by the Executive Branch.
- Norm (sociology), an informal but widely accepted _____, concept, truth, definition, or qualification (social norms, legal norms, coding norms)
- Norm (philosophy), a kind of sentence or a reason to act, feel or believe
- 'Rulership' is the concept of governance by a government:
    - Military _____, governance by a military body
    - Monastic _____, a collection of precepts that guides the life of monks or nuns in a religious order where the superior holds the place of Christ
- Slide _____

- '_____,' a song by Ayumi Hamasaki
- '_____,' a song by rapper Nas
- '_____s,' an album by the band The Whitest Boy Alive
- _____s: Pyaar Ka Superhit Formula, a 2003 Bollywood film
- ruler, an instrument for measuring lengths
- _____, a component of an astrolabe, circumferator or similar instrument
- The _____s, a bestselling self-help book
- _____ Project (Run Up-to-date Linux Everywhere), a project that aims to use up-to-date Linux software on old PCs
- _____ engine, a software system that helps managing business _____s
- Ja _____, a hip hop artist
    - R.U.L.E., a 2005 greatest hits album by rapper Ja _____
- '_____s,' a KMFDM song

a. Procter ' Gamble
b. Technocracy
c. Demand
d. Rule

9. _____s is the social science that studies the production, distribution, and consumption of goods and services. The term _____s comes from the Ancient Greek oá¼°κονομῑα from oá¼¶κος (oikos, 'house') + vÍŒμος (nomos, 'custom' or 'law'), hence 'rules of the house(hold)'. Current _____ models developed out of the broader field of political economy in the late 19th century, owing to a desire to use an empirical approach more akin to the physical sciences.
a. Inflation
b. Opportunity cost
c. Energy economics
d. Economic

Chapter 5. Urban Growth

1. _____ is a term used in economics to describe an economy where capital per worker is increasing. A process of increasing the amount of capital per worker. It is an increase in the capital intensity.
    a. Capital expenditure
    b. Capital formation
    c. Firm-specific infrastructure
    d. Capital deepening

2. _____s is the social science that studies the production, distribution, and consumption of goods and services. The term _____s comes from the Ancient Greek oá¼°κονομῖα from oá¼¶κος (oikos, 'house') + vÏŒμος (nomos, 'custom' or 'law'), hence 'rules of the house(hold)'. Current _____ models developed out of the broader field of political economy in the late 19th century, owing to a desire to use an empirical approach more akin to the physical sciences.
    a. Opportunity cost
    b. Energy economics
    c. Inflation
    d. Economic

3. _____ is the increase in the amount of the goods and services produced by an economy over time. It is conventionally measured as the percent rate of increase in real gross domestic product, or real GDP. Growth is usually calculated in real terms, i.e. inflation-adjusted terms, in order to net out the effect of inflation on the price of the goods and services produced.
    a. Economic growth
    b. ACCRA Cost of Living Index
    c. AD-IA Model
    d. ACEA agreement

4. _____ refers to the stock of skills and knowledge embodied in the ability to perform labor so as to produce economic value. It is the skills and knowledge gained by a worker through education and experience. Many early economic theories refer to it simply as labor, one of three factors of production, and consider it to be a fungible resource -- homogeneous and easily interchangeable. Other conceptions of labor dispense with these assumptions.
    a. Price theory
    b. General equilibrium
    c. Law of increasing costs
    d. Human capital

Chapter 5. Urban Growth

5. _____ is the shortage of common things such as food, clothing, shelter and safe drinking water, all of which determine the quality of life. It may also include the lack of access to opportunities such as education and employment which aid the escape from _____ and/or allow one to enjoy the respect of fellow citizens. According to Mollie Orshansky who developed the _____ measurements used by the U.S. government, 'to be poor is to be deprived of those goods and services and pleasures which others around us take for granted.' Ongoing debates over causes, effects and best ways to measure _____, directly influence the design and implementation of _____-reduction programs and are therefore relevant to the fields of public administration and international development.

   a. Poverty map
   b. Growth Elasticity of Poverty
   c. Poverty
   d. Liberal welfare reforms

6. _____s are a type of administrative division, in some countries managed by a local government. They vary greatly in size, spanning entire regions or counties, several municipalities, or subdivisions of municipalities.

   In Austria, a _____ or Bezirk is an administrative division normally encompassing several municipalities, roughly equivalent to the Landkreis in Germany.

   a. 100-year flood
   b. 130-30 fund
   c. District
   d. 1921 recession

7. The _____ is 'the basic residential unit in which economic production, consumption, inheritance, child rearing, and shelter are organized and carried out'; [the _____] 'may or may not be synonomous with family'.

   The _____ is the basic unit of analysis in many social, microeconomic and government models. The term refers to all individuals who live in the same dwelling.

   a. Household
   b. 130-30 fund
   c. Family economics
   d. 100-year flood

8. Network externalities resemble economies of scale, but they are not considered such because they are a function of the number of users of a good or service in an industry, not of the production efficiency within a business. _____ are only considered examples of network externalities if they are driven by demand side economies.

Chapter 5. Urban Growth

Formally, a production function $F(K, L)$ is defined to have:

- constant returns to scale if (for any constant a greater than or equal to 0) $F(aK, aL) = aF(K, L)$
- increasing returns to scale if (for any constant a greater than 1) $F(aK, aL) > aF(K, L)$,
- decreasing returns to scale if (for any constant a greater than 1) $F(aK, aL) < aF(K, L)$

where K and L are factors of production, capital and labour, respectively.

As an example, the Cobb-Douglas functional form has constant returns to scale when the sum of the exponents adds up to one.

a. ACCRA Cost of Living Index
b. AD-IA Model
c. ACEA agreement
d. Economies of scale external to the firm

9. In economics, an _____ is any good or commodity, transported from one country to another country in a legitimate fashion, typically for use in trade. _____ goods or services are provided to foreign consumers by domestic producers. _____ is an important part of international trade.

a. AD-IA Model
b. Export
c. ACCRA Cost of Living Index
d. ACEA agreement

10. Economics:

- _____, the desire to own something and the ability to pay for it
- _____ curve, a graphic representation of a _____ schedule
- _____ deposit, the money in checking accounts
- _____ pull theory, the theory that inflation occurs when _____ for goods and services exceeds existing supplies
- _____ schedule, a table that lists the quantity of a good a person will buy it each different price
- _____ side economics, the school of economics at believes government spending and tax cuts open economy by raising _____

a. Variability
b. McKesson ' Robbins scandal
c. Demand
d. Production

11. In economics, the _____ can be defined as the graph depicting the relationship between the price of a certain commodity, and the amount of it that consumers are willing and able to purchase at that given price. It is a graphic representation of a demand schedule. The _____ for all consumers together follows from the _____ of every individual consumer: the individual demands at each price are added together.

a. Cost curve
b. Wage curve
c. Kuznets curve
d. Demand curve

12. The supply of labor is the number of total hours that workers wish to work at a given real wage rate.

_____ curves are derived from the 'labor-leisure' trade-off. More hours worked earn higher incomes but necessitate a cut in the amount of leisure that workers enjoy.

a. Creative capitalism
b. Labor supply
c. Human trafficking
d. Late capitalism

13. _____ is an ad valorem tax that an owner is required to pay on the value of the property being taxed. _____ can be defined as 'generally, tax imposed by municipalities upon owners of property within their jurisdiction based on the value of such property.' There are three species or types of property: Land, Improvements to Land (immovable manmade objects; i.e., buildings), and Personal (movable manmade objects.) Real estate, real property or realty are all terms for the combination of land and improvements.

a. Bank regulation
b. Community property
c. Chief Financial Officers Act of 1990
d. Property tax

14. In microeconomics, _____ is quite simply the conversion of inputs into outputs. It is an economic process that uses resources to create a good or service that is suitable for exchange. This can include manufacturing, storing, shipping, and packaging.

a. Production
b. Red Guards
c. MET
d. Solved

15. _____ in economics refers to metrics and measures of output from production processes, per unit of input. Labor _____, for example, is typically measured as a ratio of output per labor-hour, an input. _____ may be conceived of as a metrics of the technical or engineering efficiency of production.

   a. Productivity
   b. Fordism
   c. Piece work
   d. Production-possibility frontier

16. To _____ is to impose a financial charge or other levy upon a taxpayer by a state or the functional equivalent of a state.

   _____es are also imposed by many subnational entities. _____es consist of direct _____ or indirect _____, and may be paid in money or as its labour equivalent (often but not always unpaid.)

   a. 130-30 fund
   b. 1921 recession
   c. 100-year flood
   d. Tax

17. To tax is to impose a financial charge or other levy upon a taxpayer by a state or the functional equivalent of a state.

   _____ are also imposed by many subnational entities. _____ consist of direct tax or indirect tax, and may be paid in money or as its labour equivalent (often but not always unpaid.)

   a. 1921 recession
   b. 130-30 fund
   c. 100-year flood
   d. Taxes

18. _____ is the cost of maintaining a certain standard of living. Changes in the _____ over time are often operationalized in a _____ index. _____ calculations are also used to compare the cost of maintaining a certain standard of living in different geographic areas.

a. Decision process tool
b. Cost of living
c. Restructuring
d. Bear raid

19. _____ can be generally defined as the course of action or inaction taken by governmental entities with regard to a particular issue or set of issues. Other scholars define it as a system of 'courses of action, regulatory measures, laws, and funding priorities concerning a given topic promulgated by a governmental entity or its representatives.' _____ is commonly embodied 'in constitutions, legislative acts, and judicial decisions.'

In the United States, this concept refers not only to the end result of policies, but more broadly to the decision-making and analysis of governmental decisions. _____ is also considered an academic discipline, as it is studied by professors and students at _____ schools of major universities throughout the country.

a. 100-year flood
b. Public policy
c. 1921 recession
d. 130-30 fund

20. _____ is a set of properties and characteristics of the environment, either generalized or local, as they impinge on human beings and other organisms.

_____ is a general term which can refer to varied characteristics that relate to the natural environment as well as the built environment, such as air and water purity or pollution, noise and the potential effects which such characteristics may have on physical and mental health caused by human activities.

In the USA the term is applied with a body of federal and state standards and regulations that are monitored by regulatory agencies.

a. ACCRA Cost of Living Index
b. Environmental quality
c. ACEA agreement
d. AD-IA Model

21. _____, short for Ecological taxation, can refer to:

A policy that introduces taxes intended to promote ecologically sustainable activities via economic incentives. Such a policy can complement or avert the need for regulatory approaches. Often, such a policy intends to maintain overall tax revenue by proportionately reducing other taxes, e.g. on human labor and renewable resources, in which case it is known as the green tax shift towards ecological taxation.

a. ACCRA Cost of Living Index
b. ACEA agreement
c. AD-IA Model
d. Ecotax

22. The Organization for Economic Co-operation and Development defines the _____ as the percentage of the working age population (ages 15 to 64 in most OECD countries) who are currently employed. According to the International Labour Organization, a person is considered employed if they have worked at least 1 hour in 'gainful' employment.

a. Employment rate
b. Informational interview
c. Underemployment
d. Encore career

23. Unemployment occurs when a person is available to work and seeking work but currently without work. The prevalence of unemployment is usually measured using the _____, which is defined as the percentage of those in the labor force who are unemployed. The _____ is also used in economic studies and economic indexes such as the United States' Conference Board's Index of Leading Indicators as a measure of the state of the macroeconomics.

a. AD-IA Model
b. Unemployment rate
c. ACCRA Cost of Living Index
d. ACEA agreement

24. _____ is a misspelled phrase from Latin 'pro capite' phrase meaning per head with pro meaning 'per' or 'for each' and capite meaning 'head.' Both words together equate to the phrase 'for each head.'

It is usually used in the field of statistics to indicate the average per person for any given concern, such as income, crime rate, etc.

It is also used in wills to indicate that each of the named beneficiaries should receive, by devise or bequest, equal shares of the estate. This is in contrast to a per stirpes division, in which each branch of the inheriting family inherits an equal share of the estate.

a. Population statistics
b. False positive rate
c. Per capita
d. Sargan test

25. In microeconomics, _____ is the extra revenue that an additional unit of product will bring. It is the additional income from selling one more unit of a good; sometimes equal to price. It can also be described as the change in total revenue/change in number of units sold.
   a. Reservation price
   b. Market demand schedule
   c. Long term
   d. Marginal revenue

26. The marginal revenue productivity theory of wages, also referred to as the _____ of labor, is the change in total revenue earned by a firm that results from employing one more unit of labor. It is a neoclassical model that determines, under some conditions, the optimal number of workers to employ at an exogenously determined market wage rate.

The _____ of a worker is equal to the product of the marginal product of labor (MP) and the marginal revenue (MR), given by MR×MP = _____.

   a. Marginal revenue productivity theory of wages
   b. Coal depletion
   c. Real prices and ideal prices
   d. Marginal revenue product

27. _____ is the provision of aid and other assistance to regions which are less economically developed. _____ may be domestic or international in nature. The implications and scope of _____ may therefore vary in accordance with the definition of a region, and how the region and its boundaries are perceived internally and externally.
   a. 130-30 fund
   b. 100-year flood
   c. Regional development
   d. Structural adjustment

28. In the study of human settlements, an _____ is an extended city or town area comprising the built-up area of a central place (usually a municipality) and any suburbs linked by continuous urban area. In France, INSEE the French Statistical Institute, translate it as 'Unité urbaine' which means continuous urbanized area. However, because of differences in definitions of what does and does not constitute an '_____', as well as variations and limitations in statistical or geographical methodology, it can be problematic to compare different _____s around the world.

a. ACCRA Cost of Living Index
b. ACEA agreement
c. AD-IA Model
d. Agglomeration

29. In economics, _____ refers to the ability of a person or a country to produce a particular good at a lower marginal cost and opportunity cost than another person or country. It is the ability to produce a product most efficiently given all the other products that could be produced. It can be contrasted with absolute advantage which refers to the ability of a person or a country to produce a particular good at a lower absolute cost than another.
a. Triffin dilemma
b. Hot money
c. Gravity model of trade
d. Comparative advantage

Chapter 6. Urban Land Rent

1. _____ is the price at which an asset would trade in a competitive Walrasian auction setting. _____ is often used interchangeably with open _____, fair value or fair _____, although these terms have distinct definitions in different standards, and may differ in some circumstances.

International Valuation Standards defines _____ as 'the estimated amount for which a property should exchange on the date of valuation between a willing buyer and a willing seller in an arm's-length transaction after proper marketing wherein the parties had each acted knowledgeably, prudently, and without compulsion.'

_____ is a concept distinct from market price, which is 'the price at which one can transact', while _____ is 'the true underlying value' according to theoretical standards.

   a. Secured loan
   b. Personal financial management
   c. Netting
   d. Market value

2. Economic _____ is defined as an excess distribution to any factor in a production process above that which is required to induce the factor into the process or any excess above that which is necessary to keep the factor in its current use..

Classical Factor _____ is primarily concerned with the fee paid for the use of fixed (e.g. natural) resources. The classical definition is expressed as any excess payment above that required to induce or provide for production.

   a. 130-30 fund
   b. 100-year flood
   c. 1921 recession
   d. Rent

3. _____ is the a method of technical and economic research of the systems for purpose to optimize a parity between system's consumer functions or properties and expenses to achieve those functions or properties.

This methodology for continuous perfection of production, industrial technologies, organizational structures was developed by Juryj Sobolev in 1948 at the 'Perm telephone factory'

- 1948 Juryj Sobolev - the first success in application of a method analysis at the 'Perm telephone factory' .
- 1949 - the first application for the invention as result of use of the new method.

Today in economically developed countries practically each enterprise or the company use methodology of the kind of functional-cost analysis as a practice of the quality management, most full satisfying to principles of standards of series ISO 9000.

- Interest of consumer not in products itself, but the advantage which it will receive from its usage.
- The consumer aspires to reduce his expenses
- Functions needed by consumer can be executed in the various ways, and, hence, with various efficiency and expenses. Among possible alternatives of realization of functions exist such in which the parity of quality and the price is the optimal for the consumer.

The goal of _____ is achievement of the highest consumer satisfaction of production at simultaneous decrease in all kinds of industrial expenses Classical _____ has three English synonyms - Value Engineering, Value Management, Value Analysis.

a. Monopoly wage
b. Staple financing
c. Willingness to pay
d. Function cost analysis

4. _____s are a type of administrative division, in some countries managed by a local government. They vary greatly in size, spanning entire regions or counties, several municipalities, or subdivisions of municipalities.

In Austria, a _____ or Bezirk is an administrative division normally encompassing several municipalities, roughly equivalent to the Landkreis in Germany.

a. 100-year flood
b. 1921 recession
c. 130-30 fund
d. District

5. _____ is a set of properties and characteristics of the environment, either generalized or local, as they impinge on human beings and other organisms.

_____ is a general term which can refer to varied characteristics that relate to the natural environment as well as the built environment, such as air and water purity or pollution, noise and the potential effects which such characteristics may have on physical and mental health caused by human activities.

In the USA the term is applied with a body of federal and state standards and regulations that are monitored by regulatory agencies.

Chapter 6. Urban Land Rent

a. AD-IA Model
b. ACEA agreement
c. ACCRA Cost of Living Index
d. Environmental quality

6. _____ in economics and business is the result of an exchange and from that trade we assign a numerical monetary value to a good, service or asset. If Alice trades Bob 4 apples for an orange, the _____ of an orange is 4 apples. Inversely, the _____ of an apple is 1/4 oranges.
   a. Price book
   b. Premium pricing
   c. Price war
   d. Price

7. In economics, an _____ is a contour line drawn through the set of points at which the same quantity of output is produced while changing the quantities of two or more inputs. While an indifference curve helps to answer the utility-maximizing problem of consumers, the _____ deals with the cost-minimization problem of producers. _____s are typically drawn on capital-labor graphs, showing the tradeoff between capital and labor in the production function, and the decreasing marginal returns of both inputs.
   a. Economies of scale
   b. Underinvestment employment relationship
   c. Economic production quantity
   d. Isoquant

8. _____ is a mechanism that allows people easily to buy and sell products. Services are often included in the scope of the term. _____ regulation is an economic term that describes restrictions in the market.
   a. Product market
   b. Financialization
   c. Market dominance
   d. Fixed exchange rate system

9. _____ is a broad label that refers to any individuals or households that use goods and services generated within the economy. The concept of a _____ is used in different contexts, so that the usage and significance of the term may vary.

Typically when business people and economists talk of _____s they are talking about person as _____, an aggregated commodity item with little individuality other than that expressed in the buy/not-buy decision.

a. Consumer
b. 100-year flood
c. 1921 recession
d. 130-30 fund

10. The _____ is 'the basic residential unit in which economic production, consumption, inheritance, child rearing, and shelter are organized and carried out'; [the _____] 'may or may not be synonomous with family'.

The _____ is the basic unit of analysis in many social, microeconomic and government models. The term refers to all individuals who live in the same dwelling.

a. Family economics
b. 100-year flood
c. Household
d. 130-30 fund

11. _____ is a measurement of population per unit area or unit volume. It is frequently applied to living organisms, and particularly to humans. It is a key term used in geography.
a. 100-year flood
b. 1921 recession
c. Population density
d. 130-30 fund

12. In probability theory, a probability _____ of a random variable is a function which describes the density of probability at each point in the sample space. The probability of a random variable falling within a given set is given by the integral of its density over the set.

A probability _____ is most commonly associated with continuous univariate distributions.

a. Memorylessness
b. Graphical model
c. Markov blanket
d. Density function

Chapter 6. Urban Land Rent

13. Economics:

    - _____, the desire to own something and the ability to pay for it
    - _____ curve, a graphic representation of a _____ schedule
    - _____ deposit, the money in checking accounts
    - _____ pull theory, the theory that inflation occurs when _____ for goods and services exceeds existing supplies
    - _____ schedule, a table that lists the quantity of a good a person will buy it each different price
    - _____ side economics, the school of economics at believes government spending and tax cuts open economy by raising _____

    a. McKesson ' Robbins scandal
    b. Variability
    c. Production
    d. Demand

14. _____ is the removal or simplification of government rules and regulations that constrain the operation of market forces. _____ does not mean elimination of laws against fraud, but eliminating or reducing government control of how business is done, thereby moving toward a more free market.

The stated rationale for '_____' is often that fewer and simpler regulations will lead to a raised level of competitiveness, therefore higher productivity, more efficiency and lower prices overall.

   a. Deregulation
   b. Fundamental psychological law
   c. Macroeconomic policy instruments
   d. Secular basis

15. In economics, the _____ is an economic law that states that consumers buy more of a good when its price decreases and less when its price increases.

There are certain goods which do not follow this law. These include Veblen and Giffen goods

   a. Market failure
   b. Financial crisis
   c. Law of demand
   d. Georgism

Chapter 6. Urban Land Rent

16. A _____ is:

- Rewrite _____, in generative grammar and computer science
- Standardization, a formal and widely-accepted statement, fact, definition, or qualification
- Operation, a determinate _____ for performing a mathematical operation and obtaining a certain result (Mathematics, Logic)
    - Unary operation
    - Binary operation
- _____ of inference, a function from sets of formulae to formulae (Mathematics, Logic)
- _____ of thumb, principle with broad application that is not intended to be strictly accurate or reliable for every situation. Also often simply referred to as a _____
- Moral, an atomic element of a moral code for guiding choices in human behavior
- Heuristic, a quantized '_____' which shows a tendency or probability for successful function
- A regulation, as in sports
- A Production _____, as in computer science
- Procedural law, a _____ set governing the application of laws to cases
    - A law, which may informally be called a '_____'
    - A court ruling, a decision by a court
- In the U.S. Government, a regulation mandated by Congress, but written or expanded upon by the Executive Branch.
- Norm (sociology), an informal but widely accepted _____, concept, truth, definition, or qualification (social norms, legal norms, coding norms)
- Norm (philosophy), a kind of sentence or a reason to act, feel or believe
- 'Rulership' is the concept of governance by a government:
    - Military _____, governance by a military body
    - Monastic _____, a collection of precepts that guides the life of monks or nuns in a religious order where the superior holds the place of Christ
- Slide _____

- '_____,' a song by Ayumi Hamasaki
- '_____,' a song by rapper Nas
- '_____s,' an album by the band The Whitest Boy Alive
- _____s: Pyaar Ka Superhit Formula, a 2003 Bollywood film
- ruler, an instrument for measuring lengths
- _____, a component of an astrolabe, circumferator or similar instrument
- The _____s, a bestselling self-help book
- _____ Project (Run Up-to-date Linux Everywhere), a project that aims to use up-to-date Linux software on old PCs
- _____ engine, a software system that helps managing business _____s
- Ja _____, a hip hop artist
    - R.U.L.E., a 2005 greatest hits album by rapper Ja _____
- '_____s,' a KMFDM song

a. Procter ' Gamble
b. Rule
c. Demand
d. Technocracy

17. In economics, the _____ or the Technical Rate of Substitution (TRS) is the amount by which the quantity of one input has to be reduced ($-\Delta x_2$) when one extra unit of another input is used ($\Delta x_1 = 1$), so that output remains constant ($y = \bar{y}$.)

$$MRTS(x_1, x_2) = \frac{\Delta x_2}{\Delta x_1} = -\frac{MP_1}{MP_2}$$

where MP_1 and MP_2 are the marginal products of input 1 and input 2, respectively.

Along an isoquant, the MRTS shows the rate at which one input (e.g. capital or labor) may be substituted for another, while maintaining the same level of output.

a. Producer surplus
b. Household production function
c. Pork cycle
d. Marginal rate of technical substitution

Chapter 7. Land-Use Patternsr

1. _____s are a type of administrative division, in some countries managed by a local government. They vary greatly in size, spanning entire regions or counties, several municipalities, or subdivisions of municipalities.

In Austria, a _____ or Bezirk is an administrative division normally encompassing several municipalities, roughly equivalent to the Landkreis in Germany.

   a. 100-year flood
   b. 1921 recession
   c. District
   d. 130-30 fund

2. A _____ is the procedure of systematically acquiring and recording information about the members of a given population. It is a regularly occurring and official count of a particular population. The term is used mostly in connection with national 'population and door to door _____es' (to be taken every 10 years according to United Nations recommendations), agriculture, and business _____es.
   a. 100-year flood
   b. 130-30 fund
   c. 1921 recession
   d. Census

3. _____ is an American term for a concentration of business, shopping, and entertainment outside a traditional urban area in what had recently been a residential suburb or semi-rural community. The term was first used in Tom Wolfe's 1968 novel The Electric Kool-Aid Acid Test and popularized in the 1991 book _____: Life on the New Frontier by Joel Garreau, who established its current meaning while working as a reporter for the Washington Post. Garreau argues that the _____ has become the standard form of urban growth worldwide, representing a 20th-century urban form unlike that of the 19th-century central downtown.
   a. ACCRA Cost of Living Index
   b. ACEA agreement
   c. AD-IA Model
   d. Edge city

4. _____ is a measurement of population per unit area or unit volume. It is frequently applied to living organisms, and particularly to humans. It is a key term used in geography.
   a. 100-year flood
   b. Population density
   c. 130-30 fund
   d. 1921 recession

5. In probability theory, a probability _____ of a random variable is a function which describes the density of probability at each point in the sample space. The probability of a random variable falling within a given set is given by the integral of its density over the set.

A probability _____ is most commonly associated with continuous univariate distributions.

   a. Density function
   b. Markov blanket
   c. Memorylessness
   d. Graphical model

6. In vector calculus, the _____ of a scalar field is a vector field which points in the direction of the greatest rate of increase of the scalar field, and whose magnitude is the greatest rate of change.

A generalization of the _____ for functions on a Euclidean space which have values in another Euclidean space is the Jacobian. A further generalization for a function from one Banach space to another is the Fréchet derivative.

   a. 130-30 fund
   b. 1921 recession
   c. 100-year flood
   d. Gradient

7. In microeconomics, _____ is quite simply the conversion of inputs into outputs. It is an economic process that uses resources to create a good or service that is suitable for exchange. This can include manufacturing, storing, shipping, and packaging.
   a. MET
   b. Solved
   c. Red Guards
   d. Production

8. _____ is a term used in urban planning and urban design to refer to the number of people inhabiting a given urbanized area. As such it is to be distinguished from other measures of population density. _____ is considered an important factor in understanding how cities function.
   a. Urbanization
   b. Urban prairie
   c. Urban density
   d. ACCRA Cost of Living Index

9. _____, in microeconomics, are the cost advantages that a business obtains due to expansion. They are factors that cause a producere;s average cost per unit to fall as scale is increased. _____ is a long run concept and refers to reductions in unit cost as the size of a facility, or scale, increases.

   a. Isoquant
   b. Economies of scale
   c. Underinvestment employment relationship
   d. Economic production quantity

10. The _____ was a period in the late 18th and early 19th centuries when major changes in agriculture, manufacturing, mining, and transportation had a profound effect on the socioeconomic and cultural conditions in Britain. The changes subsequently spread throughout Europe, North America, and eventually the world. The onset of the _____ marked a major turning point in human society; almost every aspect of daily life was eventually influenced in some way.

   a. Adolph Fischer
   b. Adolf Hitler
   c. Adam Smith
   d. Industrial Revolution

11. _____ is the removal or simplification of government rules and regulations that constrain the operation of market forces. _____ does not mean elimination of laws against fraud, but eliminating or reducing government control of how business is done, thereby moving toward a more free market.

The stated rationale for '_____' is often that fewer and simpler regulations will lead to a raised level of competitiveness, therefore higher productivity, more efficiency and lower prices overall.

   a. Deregulation
   b. Fundamental psychological law
   c. Secular basis
   d. Macroeconomic policy instruments

12. In the study of human settlements, an _____ is an extended city or town area comprising the built-up area of a central place (usually a municipality) and any suburbs linked by continuous urban area. In France, INSEE the French Statistical Institute, translate it as 'Unité urbaine' which means continuous urbanized area. However, because of differences in definitions of what does and does not constitute an '_____', as well as variations and limitations in statistical or geographical methodology, it can be problematic to compare different _____s around the world.

   a. ACEA agreement
   b. ACCRA Cost of Living Index
   c. AD-IA Model
   d. Agglomeration

Chapter 7. Land-Use Patternsr

13. _____ is a term used to describe the process of population movement from within towns and cities to the rural-urban fringe. It is one of the many causes of the increase in urban sprawl. Many residents of metropolitan areas no longer live and work within the central urban area, choosing instead to live in satellite communities called suburbs and commute to work via automobile or mass transit.
   a. Suburbanization
   b. 100-year flood
   c. Rural exodus
   d. Redevelopment

14. _____ is the shortage of common things such as food, clothing, shelter and safe drinking water, all of which determine the quality of life. It may also include the lack of access to opportunities such as education and employment which aid the escape from _____ and/or allow one to enjoy the respect of fellow citizens. According to Mollie Orshansky who developed the _____ measurements used by the U.S. government, 'to be poor is to be deprived of those goods and services and pleasures which others around us take for granted.' Ongoing debates over causes, effects and best ways to measure _____, directly influence the design and implementation of _____-reduction programs and are therefore relevant to the fields of public administration and international development.
   a. Growth Elasticity of Poverty
   b. Liberal welfare reforms
   c. Poverty map
   d. Poverty

15. Economics:

   - _____,the desire to own something and the ability to pay for it
   - _____ curve,a graphic representation of a _____ schedule
   - _____ deposit, the money in checking accounts
   - _____ pull theory,the theory that inflation occurs when _____ for goods and services exceeds existing supplies
   - _____ schedule,a table that lists the quantity of a good a person will buy it each different price
   - _____ side economics,the school of economics at believes government spending and tax cuts open economy by raising _____

   a. Demand
   b. McKesson ' Robbins scandal
   c. Production
   d. Variability

16. The _____ is 'the basic residential unit in which economic production, consumption, inheritance, child rearing, and shelter are organized and carried out'; [the _____] 'may or may not be synonymous with family'.

The _____ is the basic unit of analysis in many social, microeconomic and government models. The term refers to all individuals who live in the same dwelling.

   a. 130-30 fund
   b. Household
   c. 100-year flood
   d. Family economics

17. A _____ is a bond which is worth a certain monetary value and which may only be spent for specific reasons or on specific goods. Examples include -- but are not limited to -- housing, travel and food _____s. The term _____ is also a synonym for receipt, and is often used to refer to receipts used as evidence of, for example, the declaration that a service has been performed or that an expenditure has been made.
   a. 1921 recession
   b. Voucher
   c. 100-year flood
   d. 130-30 fund

18. _____ refers to the stock of skills and knowledge embodied in the ability to perform labor so as to produce economic value. It is the skills and knowledge gained by a worker through education and experience. Many early economic theories refer to it simply as labor, one of three factors of production, and consider it to be a fungible resource -- homogeneous and easily interchangeable. Other conceptions of labor dispense with these assumptions.
   a. Law of increasing costs
   b. Human capital
   c. Price theory
   d. General equilibrium

19. _____ is the spreading of a city and its suburbs over rural land at the fringe of an urban area. Residents of sprawling neighborhoods tend to live in single-family homes and commute by automobile to work. Low population density is an indicator of sprawl.
   a. ACEA agreement
   b. ACCRA Cost of Living Index
   c. AD-IA Model
   d. Urban sprawl

Chapter 7. Land-Use Patternsr

20. The term _____ refers to government debt, expenditures and revenues, or to finance (particularly financial revenue) in general.

- _____ deficit is the budget deficit of federal or local government
- _____ policy is the discretionary spending of governments. Contrasts with monetary policy.
- _____ year and _____ quarter are reporting periods for firms and other agencies.

a. Fiscal
b. Bucket shop
c. Drawdown
d. Procter ' Gamble

21. _____ is the application of economic techniques to real estate markets. It tries to describe, explain, and predict patterns of prices, supply, and demand. The closely related fields of housing economics is narrower in scope, concentrating on residential real estate markets as does the research of real estate trends focus on the business and structural changes impacting the industry.
a. 130-30 fund
b. Real estate economics
c. 1921 recession
d. 100-year flood

22. _____ is an ad valorem tax that an owner is required to pay on the value of the property being taxed. _____ can be defined as 'generally, tax imposed by municipalities upon owners of property within their jurisdiction based on the value of such property.' There are three species or types of property: Land, Improvements to Land (immovable manmade objects; i.e., buildings), and Personal (movable manmade objects.) Real estate, real property or realty are all terms for the combination of land and improvements.
a. Community property
b. Bank regulation
c. Chief Financial Officers Act of 1990
d. Property tax

23. _____ is a form of housing tenure in which the property is owned by a government authority, which may be central or local. Social housing is an umbrella term referring to rental housing which may be owned and managed by the state, by not-for-profit organizations, or by a combination of the two, usually with the aim of providing affordable housing.

Although the common goal of _____ is to provide affordable housing, the details, terminology, definitions of poverty and other criteria for allocation vary.

a. 130-30 fund
b. 100-year flood
c. 1921 recession
d. Public housing

24. _____ can be generally defined as the course of action or inaction taken by governmental entities with regard to a particular issue or set of issues. Other scholars define it as a system of 'courses of action, regulatory measures, laws, and funding priorities concerning a given topic promulgated by a governmental entity or its representatives.' _____ is commonly embodied 'in constitutions, legislative acts, and judicial decisions.'

In the United States, this concept refers not only to the end result of policies, but more broadly to the decision-making and analysis of governmental decisions. _____ is also considered an academic discipline, as it is studied by professors and students at _____ schools of major universities throughout the country.

a. 1921 recession
b. 100-year flood
c. Public policy
d. 130-30 fund

25. Necessary _____s:

If x is a necessary _____ of y, then the presence of y necessarily implies the presence of x. The presence of x, however, does not imply that y will occur.

Sufficient _____s:

If x is a sufficient _____ of y, then the presence of x necessarily implies the presence of y.

a. Materialism
b. Philosophy of economics
c. Political philosophy
d. Cause

26. In economics, _____ is the ratio of the percent change in one variable to the percent change in another variable. It is a tool for measuring the responsiveness of a function to changes in parameters in a relative way. Commonly analyzed are _____ of substitution, price and wealth.

a. ACCRA Cost of Living Index
b. ACEA agreement
c. Elasticity
d. Elasticity of demand

27. Price _____ is defined as the measure of responsiveness in the quantity demanded for a commodity as a result of change in price of the same commodity. It is a measure of how consumers react to a change in price. In other words, it is percentage change in quantity demanded by the percentage change in price of the same commodity.
   a. ACCRA Cost of Living Index
   b. Elasticity
   c. ACEA agreement
   d. Elasticity of demand

28. _____ is a fee paid on borrowed assets. It is the price paid for the use of borrowed money , or, money earned by deposited funds . Assets that are sometimes lent with _____ include money, shares, consumer goods through hire purchase, major assets such as aircraft, and even entire factories in finance lease arrangements.
   a. Internal debt
   b. Insolvency
   c. Asset protection
   d. Interest

29. To _____ is to impose a financial charge or other levy upon a taxpayer by a state or the functional equivalent of a state.

_____es are also imposed by many subnational entities. _____es consist of direct _____ or indirect _____, and may be paid in money or as its labour equivalent (often but not always unpaid.)

   a. 100-year flood
   b. 1921 recession
   c. Tax
   d. 130-30 fund

30. To tax is to impose a financial charge or other levy upon a taxpayer by a state or the functional equivalent of a state.

_____ are also imposed by many subnational entities. _____ consist of direct tax or indirect tax, and may be paid in money or as its labour equivalent (often but not always unpaid.)

a. 130-30 fund
b. 1921 recession
c. 100-year flood
d. Taxes

31. _____ is a set of properties and characteristics of the environment, either generalized or local, as they impinge on human beings and other organisms.

_____ is a general term which can refer to varied characteristics that relate to the natural environment as well as the built environment, such as air and water purity or pollution, noise and the potential effects which such characteristics may have on physical and mental health caused by human activities.

In the USA the term is applied with a body of federal and state standards and regulations that are monitored by regulatory agencies.

a. ACEA agreement
b. ACCRA Cost of Living Index
c. Environmental quality
d. AD-IA Model

32. _____, or a _____ is the concept of a resulting effect (cf. cause and effect, arising from another action. In general terms, it is used to indicate that all human actions, particularly crime and sin, have profound effects.
a. Variability
b. Solved
c. Rule
d. Consequence

33. _____ is a common concept in economics, and gives rise to derived concepts such as consumer debt. Generally _____ is defined by opposition to production. But the precise definition can vary because different schools of economists define production quite differently.
a. Cash or share options
b. Foreclosure data providers
c. Consumption
d. Federal Reserve Bank Notes

34. _____ is a mechanism that allows people easily to buy and sell products. Services are often included in the scope of the term. _____ regulation is an economic term that describes restrictions in the market.

a. Fixed exchange rate system
b. Financialization
c. Product market
d. Market dominance

35. _____ in economics and business is the result of an exchange and from that trade we assign a numerical monetary value to a good, service or asset. If Alice trades Bob 4 apples for an orange, the _____ of an orange is 4 apples. Inversely, the _____ of an apple is 1/4 oranges.
   a. Premium pricing
   b. Price
   c. Price book
   d. Price war

36. Economic _____ is defined as an excess distribution to any factor in a production process above that which is required to induce the factor into the process or any excess above that which is necessary to keep the factor in its current use..

Classical Factor _____ is primarily concerned with the fee paid for the use of fixed (e.g. natural) resources. The classical definition is expressed as any excess payment above that required to induce or provide for production.

   a. 130-30 fund
   b. 1921 recession
   c. 100-year flood
   d. Rent

Chapter 8. Neighborhood Choice

1. _____ is the shortage of common things such as food, clothing, shelter and safe drinking water, all of which determine the quality of life. It may also include the lack of access to opportunities such as education and employment which aid the escape from _____ and/or allow one to enjoy the respect of fellow citizens. According to Mollie Orshansky who developed the _____ measurements used by the U.S. government, 'to be poor is to be deprived of those goods and services and pleasures which others around us take for granted.' Ongoing debates over causes, effects and best ways to measure _____, directly influence the design and implementation of _____-reduction programs and are therefore relevant to the fields of public administration and international development.

   a. Liberal welfare reforms
   b. Poverty
   c. Poverty map
   d. Growth Elasticity of Poverty

2. _____s are a type of administrative division, in some countries managed by a local government. They vary greatly in size, spanning entire regions or counties, several municipalities, or subdivisions of municipalities.

   In Austria, a _____ or Bezirk is an administrative division normally encompassing several municipalities, roughly equivalent to the Landkreis in Germany.

   a. 1921 recession
   b. 100-year flood
   c. District
   d. 130-30 fund

3. The _____ is 'the basic residential unit in which economic production, consumption, inheritance, child rearing, and shelter are organized and carried out'; [the _____] 'may or may not be synonymous with family'.

   The _____ is the basic unit of analysis in many social, microeconomic and government models. The term refers to all individuals who live in the same dwelling.

   a. Family economics
   b. Household
   c. 130-30 fund
   d. 100-year flood

4. A _____ is the procedure of systematically acquiring and recording information about the members of a given population. It is a regularly occurring and official count of a particular population. The term is used mostly in connection with national 'population and door to door _____es' (to be taken every 10 years according to United Nations recommendations), agriculture, and business _____es.

Chapter 8. Neighborhood Choice 49

   a. 100-year flood
   b. 130-30 fund
   c. 1921 recession
   d. Census

5. _____ is an ad valorem tax that an owner is required to pay on the value of the property being taxed. _____ can be defined as 'generally, tax imposed by municipalities upon owners of property within their jurisdiction based on the value of such property.' There are three species or types of property: Land, Improvements to Land (immovable manmade objects; i.e., buildings), and Personal (movable manmade objects.) Real estate, real property or realty are all terms for the combination of land and improvements.
   a. Chief Financial Officers Act of 1990
   b. Property tax
   c. Community property
   d. Bank regulation

6. The _____ Tiebout migration is a public choice theory model first described by economist Charles Tiebout in his article 'A Pure Theory of Local Expenditures' The essence of the model is that there is in fact a non-political solution to the free rider problem in local governance.

Tiebout first proposed the model informally as a graduate student in a seminar with Richard Musgrave, who argued that the free rider problem necessarily required a political solution.

   a. 1921 recession
   b. 100-year flood
   c. 130-30 fund
   d. Tiebout model

7. _____ is a set of properties and characteristics of the environment, either generalized or local, as they impinge on human beings and other organisms.

_____ is a general term which can refer to varied characteristics that relate to the natural environment as well as the built environment, such as air and water purity or pollution, noise and the potential effects which such characteristics may have on physical and mental health caused by human activities.

In the USA the term is applied with a body of federal and state standards and regulations that are monitored by regulatory agencies.

Chapter 8. Neighborhood Choice

a. AD-IA Model
b. ACEA agreement
c. ACCRA Cost of Living Index
d. Environmental quality

8. A _____ is an object whose consumption increases the utility of the consumer, for which the quantity demanded exceeds the quantity supplied at zero price. _____s are usually modeled as having diminishing marginal utility. The first individual purchase has high utility; the second has less.

a. Composite good
b. Pie method
c. Good
d. Merit good

9. In economics, a _____ is a good that is non-rivaled and non-excludable. This means, respectively, that consumption of the good by one individual does not reduce availability of the good for consumption by others; and that no one can be effectively excluded from using the good. In the real world, there may be no such thing as an absolutely non-rivaled and non-excludable good; but economists think that some goods approximate the concept closely enough for the analysis to be economically useful.

a. Demand-pull theory
b. Happiness economics
c. Neoclassical synthesis
d. Public good

10. To _____ is to impose a financial charge or other levy upon a taxpayer by a state or the functional equivalent of a state.

_____es are also imposed by many subnational entities. _____es consist of direct _____ or indirect _____, and may be paid in money or as its labour equivalent (often but not always unpaid.)

a. Tax
b. 100-year flood
c. 130-30 fund
d. 1921 recession

11. To tax is to impose a financial charge or other levy upon a taxpayer by a state or the functional equivalent of a state.

_____ are also imposed by many subnational entities. _____ consist of direct tax or indirect tax, and may be paid in money or as its labour equivalent (often but not always unpaid.)

a. Taxes
b. 100-year flood
c. 1921 recession
d. 130-30 fund

12. Economics:

    - _____, the desire to own something and the ability to pay for it
    - _____ curve, a graphic representation of a _____ schedule
    - _____ deposit, the money in checking accounts
    - _____ pull theory, the theory that inflation occurs when _____ for goods and services exceeds existing supplies
    - _____ schedule, a table that lists the quantity of a good a person will buy it each different price
    - _____ side economics, the school of economics at believes government spending and tax cuts open economy by raising _____

a. McKesson ' Robbins scandal
b. Production
c. Variability
d. Demand

13. _____ has several particular meanings:

    - in mathematics
        - _____ function
        - Euler _____
        - _____
        - _____ subgroup
        - method of _____s (partial differential equations)
    - in physics and engineering
        - any _____ curve that shows the relationship between certain input- and output parameters, e.g.
        - an I-V or current-voltage _____ is the current in a circuit as a function of the applied voltage
        - Receiver-Operator _____
    - in fiction
        - in Dungeons ' Dragons, _____ is another name for ability score

a. Characteristic
b. Russian financial crisis
c. Demand
d. Technocracy

14. A _____ is:

- Rewrite _____, in generative grammar and computer science
- Standardization, a formal and widely-accepted statement, fact, definition, or qualification
- Operation, a determinate _____ for performing a mathematical operation and obtaining a certain result (Mathematics, Logic)
    - Unary operation
    - Binary operation
- _____ of inference, a function from sets of formulae to formulae (Mathematics, Logic)
- _____ of thumb, principle with broad application that is not intended to be strictly accurate or reliable for every situation. Also often simply referred to as a _____
- Moral, an atomic element of a moral code for guiding choices in human behavior
- Heuristic, a quantized '_____' which shows a tendency or probability for successful function
- A regulation, as in sports
- A Production _____, as in computer science
- Procedural law, a _____ set governing the application of laws to cases
    - A law, which may informally be called a '_____'
    - A court ruling, a decision by a court
- In the U.S. Government, a regulation mandated by Congress, but written or expanded upon by the Executive Branch.
- Norm (sociology), an informal but widely accepted _____, concept, truth, definition, or qualification (social norms, legal norms, coding norms)
- Norm (philosophy), a kind of sentence or a reason to act, feel or believe
- 'Rulership' is the concept of governance by a government:
    - Military _____, governance by a military body
    - Monastic _____, a collection of precepts that guides the life of monks or nuns in a religious order where the superior holds the place of Christ
- Slide _____

- '_____,' a song by Ayumi Hamasaki
- '_____,' a song by rapper Nas
- '_____s,' an album by the band The Whitest Boy Alive
- _____s: Pyaar Ka Superhit Formula, a 2003 Bollywood film
- ruler, an instrument for measuring lengths
- _____, a component of an astrolabe, circumferator or similar instrument
- The _____s, a bestselling self-help book
- _____ Project (Run Up-to-date Linux Everywhere), a project that aims to use up-to-date Linux software on old PCs
- _____ engine, a software system that helps managing business _____s
- Ja _____, a hip hop artist
    - R.U.L.E., a 2005 greatest hits album by rapper Ja _____
- '_____s,' a KMFDM song

a. Demand
b. Rule
c. Procter ' Gamble
d. Technocracy

15. _____ is a common concept in economics, and gives rise to derived concepts such as consumer debt. Generally _____ is defined by opposition to production. But the precise definition can vary because different schools of economists define production quite differently.

a. Federal Reserve Bank Notes
b. Consumption
c. Foreclosure data providers
d. Cash or share options

16. A municipality is an administrative entity composed of a clearly defined territory and its population and commonly denotes a city, town or a small grouping of them. A municipality is typically governed by a mayor and a city council or _____ council.

The notion of municipality includes townships but is not restricted to them.

a. Municipal
b. 100-year flood
c. 1921 recession
d. 130-30 fund

17. In the study of human settlements, an _____ is an extended city or town area comprising the built-up area of a central place (usually a municipality) and any suburbs linked by continuous urban area. In France, INSEE the French Statistical Institute, translate it as 'Unité urbaine' which means continuous urbanized area. However, because of differences in definitions of what does and does not constitute an '_____', as well as variations and limitations in statistical or geographical methodology, it can be problematic to compare different _____s around the world.

a. ACCRA Cost of Living Index
b. ACEA agreement
c. AD-IA Model
d. Agglomeration

18. Many _____ are related to the environmental consequences of production and use

- Systemic risk describes the risks to the overall economy arising from the risks which the banking system takes. That the private costs of banking failure may be smaller than the social costs justifies banking regulations, although regulations could create a moral hazard.

- Anthropogenic climate change is attributed to greenhouse gas emissions from burning oil, gas, and coal. Global warming has been ranked as the #1 externality of all economic activity, in the magnitude of potential harms and yet remains unmitigated.

a. Negative Externalities
b. Green certificate
c. Total Economic Value
d. White certificates

19. Examples of _____ include:

- A beekeeper keeps the bees for their honey. A side effect or externality associated with his activity is the pollination of surrounding crops by the bees. The value generated by the pollination may be more important than the value of the harvested honey.

- An individual planting an attractive garden in front of his house may provide benefits to others living in the area, and even financial benefits in the form of increased property values for all property owners.

- An individual buying a product that is interconnected in a network (e.g., a video cellphone) will increase the usefulness of such phones to other people who have a video cellphone. When each new user of a product increases the value of the same product owned by others, the phenomenon is called a network externality or a network effect. Network externalities often have 'tipping points' where, suddenly, the product reaches general acceptance and near-universal usage, a phenomenon which can be seen in the near universal take-up of cellphones in some Scandinavian countries.

- Knowledge spillover of inventions and information - once an invention (or most other forms of practical information) is discovered or made more easily accessible, others benefit by exploiting the invention or information. Copyright and intellectual property law are mechanisms to allow the inventor or creator to benefit from a temporary, state-protected monopoly in return for 'sharing' the information through publication or other means.

a. Negative externalities
b. Positive Externalities
c. Total Economic Value
d. Weighted average cost of carbon

20. _____ can be generally defined as the course of action or inaction taken by governmental entities with regard to a particular issue or set of issues. Other scholars define it as a system of 'courses of action, regulatory measures, laws, and funding priorities concerning a given topic promulgated by a governmental entity or its representatives.' _____ is commonly embodied 'in constitutions, legislative acts, and judicial decisions.'

In the United States, this concept refers not only to the end result of policies, but more broadly to the decision-making and analysis of governmental decisions. _____ is also considered an academic discipline, as it is studied by professors and students at _____ schools of major universities throughout the country.

   a. 130-30 fund
   b. 100-year flood
   c. 1921 recession
   d. Public policy

21. _____ refers to the stock of skills and knowledge embodied in the ability to perform labor so as to produce economic value. It is the skills and knowledge gained by a worker through education and experience. Many early economic theories refer to it simply as labor, one of three factors of production, and consider it to be a fungible resource -- homogeneous and easily interchangeable. Other conceptions of labor dispense with these assumptions.
   a. Price theory
   b. General equilibrium
   c. Law of increasing costs
   d. Human capital

22. _____ in economics and business is the result of an exchange and from that trade we assign a numerical monetary value to a good, service or asset. If Alice trades Bob 4 apples for an orange, the _____ of an orange is 4 apples. Inversely, the _____ of an apple is 1/4 oranges.
   a. Premium pricing
   b. Price war
   c. Price
   d. Price book

23. A _____ is a place of residence or refuge and comfort. It is usually a place in which an individual or a family can rest and be able to store personal property. Most modern-day households contain sanitary facilities and a means of preparing food.
   a. 100-year flood
   b. Home
   c. 1921 recession
   d. 130-30 fund

24. _____ or the economics of education is the study of economic issues relating to education, including the the demand for education and the financing and provision of education.

The dominant model of the demand for education is based on human capital theory. The central idea is that undertaking education is investment in the acquisition of skills and knowledge which will increase earnings, or provide longterm benefits such as an appreciation of literature .

   a. ACCRA Cost of Living Index
   b. Education economics
   c. ACEA agreement
   d. AD-IA Model

25. In microeconomics, _____ is quite simply the conversion of inputs into outputs. It is an economic process that uses resources to create a good or service that is suitable for exchange. This can include manufacturing, storing, shipping, and packaging.
   a. Production
   b. Solved
   c. Red Guards
   d. MET

26. In economics, a _____ is a function that specifies the output of a firm, an industry, or an entire economy for all combinations of inputs. A meta-_____ compares the practice of the existing entities converting inputs X into output y to determine the most efficient practice _____ of the existing entities, whether the most efficient feasible practice production or the most efficient actual practice production. In either case, the maximum output of a technologically-determined production process is a mathematical function of input factors of production.
   a. Constant elasticity of substitution
   b. Post-Fordism
   c. Short-run
   d. Production function

27. The '_____' is a demographic measure of the evenness with which two groups are distributed across the component geographic areas that make up a larger area. The index score can also be interpreted as the percentage of one of the two groups included in the calculation that would have to move to different geographic areas in order to produce a completely even distribution. The _____ can also be used as a measure of inequality.
   a. Index of diversity
   b. Index of Leading Indicators
   c. Atkinson index
   d. Index of dissimilarity

Chapter 8. Neighborhood Choice

28. Necessary _____s:

If x is a necessary _____ of y, then the presence of y necessarily implies the presence of x. The presence of x, however, does not imply that y will occur.

Sufficient _____s:

If x is a sufficient _____ of y, then the presence of x necessarily implies the presence of y.

   a. Political philosophy
   b. Philosophy of economics
   c. Cause
   d. Materialism

29. _____ is a form of housing tenure in which the property is owned by a government authority, which may be central or local. Social housing is an umbrella term referring to rental housing which may be owned and managed by the state, by not-for-profit organizations, or by a combination of the two, usually with the aim of providing affordable housing.

Although the common goal of _____ is to provide affordable housing, the details, terminology, definitions of poverty and other criteria for allocation vary.

   a. 100-year flood
   b. 1921 recession
   c. Public housing
   d. 130-30 fund

30. _____ is the sociological, economic and political phenomenon associated with economic restructuring in which employment opportunities for low-income people are located far away from the areas where they live. In the United States, this takes the form of high concentrations of poverty in central cities, with low-wage, low-skill employment opportunities concentrated in the suburbs.

The term was first used by John F. Kain in 1968.

   a. Day job
   b. Hygiene factors
   c. Supported employment
   d. Spatial mismatch

31. A _____ is a party that mediates between a buyer and a seller. A _____ who also acts as a seller or as a buyer becomes a principal party to the deal. Distinguish agent: one who acts on behalf of a principal.
   a. Broker
   b. Primary labor market
   c. Full-time
   d. No call, no show

32. _____, or a _____ is the concept of a resulting effect (cf. cause and effect, arising from another action. In general terms, it is used to indicate that all human actions, particularly crime and sin, have profound effects.
   a. Consequence
   b. Variability
   c. Solved
   d. Rule

33. The Organization for Economic Co-operation and Development defines the _____ as the percentage of the working age population (ages 15 to 64 in most OECD countries) who are currently employed. According to the International Labour Organization, a person is considered employed if they have worked at least 1 hour in 'gainful' employment.
   a. Underemployment
   b. Informational interview
   c. Encore career
   d. Employment rate

34. In a federal system of government, a _____ is a large sum of money granted by the national government to a regional government with only general provisions as to the way it is to be spent. This can be contrasted with a categorical grant which has more strict and specific provisions on the way it is to be spent.

An advantage of _____s is that they allow regional governments to experiment with different ways of spending money with the same goal in mind, though it is very difficult to compare the results of such spending and reach a conclusion.

   a. Transactions deposit
   b. Financial Industry Regulatory Authority
   c. 100-year flood
   d. Block Grant

35. _____ is a term used to describe the process of population movement from within towns and cities to the rural-urban fringe. It is one of the many causes of the increase in urban sprawl. Many residents of metropolitan areas no longer live and work within the central urban area, choosing instead to live in satellite communities called suburbs and commute to work via automobile or mass transit.
   a. Suburbanization
   b. 100-year flood
   c. Redevelopment
   d. Rural exodus

36. _____ is the application of economic techniques to real estate markets. It tries to describe, explain, and predict patterns of prices, supply, and demand. The closely related fields of housing economics is narrower in scope, concentrating on residential real estate markets as does the research of real estate trends focus on the business and structural changes impacting the industry.
   a. 1921 recession
   b. Real estate economics
   c. 100-year flood
   d. 130-30 fund

37. A _____ is a scenario 'in which a poor country is simply too poor to achieve sustained economic growth.' The trap becomes cyclical and begins to reinforce itself if steps are not taken to break the cycle. Depending upon a person;s origin of birth, they may find themselves financially stable their entire lives, or at the other extreme, they may find themselves born into severe poverty that seems utterly inescapable. Many factors contribute to a _____, and these factors vary from case to case.
   a. Adam Smith
   b. Adolph Fischer
   c. Poverty trap
   d. Adolf Hitler

Chapter 9. Zoning and Growth Controls

1. An _____ is a regional boundary, set in an attempt to control urban sprawl by mandating that the area inside the boundary be used for higher density urban development and the area outside be used for lower density development.

An _____ circumscribes an entire urbanized area and is used by local governments as a guide to zoning and land use decisions. If the area affected by the boundary includes multiple jurisdictions a special urban planning agency may be created by the state or regional government to manage the boundary.

   a. Urban growth boundary
   b. ACEA agreement
   c. Income approach
   d. ACCRA Cost of Living Index

2. In the study of human settlements, an _____ is an extended city or town area comprising the built-up area of a central place (usually a municipality) and any suburbs linked by continuous urban area. In France, INSEE the French Statistical Institute, translate it as 'Unité urbaine' which means continuous urbanized area. However, because of differences in definitions of what does and does not constitute an '_____', as well as variations and limitations in statistical or geographical methodology, it can be problematic to compare different _____s around the world.
   a. AD-IA Model
   b. Agglomeration
   c. ACCRA Cost of Living Index
   d. ACEA agreement

3. _____ is a set of properties and characteristics of the environment, either generalized or local, as they impinge on human beings and other organisms.

_____ is a general term which can refer to varied characteristics that relate to the natural environment as well as the built environment, such as air and water purity or pollution, noise and the potential effects which such characteristics may have on physical and mental health caused by human activities.

In the USA the term is applied with a body of federal and state standards and regulations that are monitored by regulatory agencies.

   a. ACEA agreement
   b. ACCRA Cost of Living Index
   c. AD-IA Model
   d. Environmental quality

4. _____ is the removal or simplification of government rules and regulations that constrain the operation of market forces. _____ does not mean elimination of laws against fraud, but eliminating or reducing government control of how business is done, thereby moving toward a more free market.

Chapter 9. Zoning and Growth Controls

The stated rationale for '_____' is often that fewer and simpler regulations will lead to a raised level of competitiveness, therefore higher productivity, more efficiency and lower prices overall.

  a. Deregulation
  b. Secular basis
  c. Macroeconomic policy instruments
  d. Fundamental psychological law

5. _____ is any (course of) action deliberately taken (or not taken) to manage human activities with a view to prevent, reduce or mitigate harmful effects on nature and natural resources, and ensuring that man-made changes to the environment do not have harmful effects on humans.

It is useful to consider that _____ comprises two major terms: environment and policy. Environment primarily refers to the ecological (ecosystems) dimension, but can also take account of social (quality of life) dimension and an economic (resource management) dimension.

  a. Environmental policy
  b. AD-IA Model
  c. ACEA agreement
  d. ACCRA Cost of Living Index

6. The term _____ refers to government debt, expenditures and revenues, or to finance (particularly financial revenue) in general.

- _____ deficit is the budget deficit of federal or local government
- _____ policy is the discretionary spending of governments. Contrasts with monetary policy.
- _____ year and _____ quarter are reporting periods for firms and other agencies.

  a. Drawdown
  b. Procter ' Gamble
  c. Bucket shop
  d. Fiscal

Chapter 9. Zoning and Growth Controls

7. _____ is the shortage of common things such as food, clothing, shelter and safe drinking water, all of which determine the quality of life. It may also include the lack of access to opportunities such as education and employment which aid the escape from _____ and/or allow one to enjoy the respect of fellow citizens. According to Mollie Orshansky who developed the _____ measurements used by the U.S. government, 'to be poor is to be deprived of those goods and services and pleasures which others around us take for granted.' Ongoing debates over causes, effects and best ways to measure _____, directly influence the design and implementation of _____-reduction programs and are therefore relevant to the fields of public administration and international development.

   a. Poverty map
   b. Poverty
   c. Growth Elasticity of Poverty
   d. Liberal welfare reforms

8. _____ is an ad valorem tax that an owner is required to pay on the value of the property being taxed. _____ can be defined as 'generally, tax imposed by municipalities upon owners of property within their jurisdiction based on the value of such property.' There are three species or types of property: Land, Improvements to Land (immovable manmade objects; i.e., buildings), and Personal (movable manmade objects.) Real estate, real property or realty are all terms for the combination of land and improvements.

   a. Property tax
   b. Community property
   c. Bank regulation
   d. Chief Financial Officers Act of 1990

9. _____ is a form of housing tenure in which the property is owned by a government authority, which may be central or local. Social housing is an umbrella term referring to rental housing which may be owned and managed by the state, by not-for-profit organizations, or by a combination of the two, usually with the aim of providing affordable housing.

Although the common goal of _____ is to provide affordable housing, the details, terminology, definitions of poverty and other criteria for allocation vary.

   a. 130-30 fund
   b. 100-year flood
   c. Public housing
   d. 1921 recession

10. The _____ is 'the basic residential unit in which economic production, consumption, inheritance, child rearing, and shelter are organized and carried out'; [the _____] 'may or may not be synonymous with family'.

The _____ is the basic unit of analysis in many social, microeconomic and government models. The term refers to all individuals who live in the same dwelling.

Chapter 9. Zoning and Growth Controls

a. Family economics
b. 100-year flood
c. 130-30 fund
d. Household

11. _____, short for Ecological taxation, can refer to:

A policy that introduces taxes intended to promote ecologically sustainable activities via economic incentives. Such a policy can complement or avert the need for regulatory approaches. Often, such a policy intends to maintain overall tax revenue by proportionately reducing other taxes, e.g. on human labor and renewable resources, in which case it is known as the green tax shift towards ecological taxation.

a. AD-IA Model
b. ACEA agreement
c. ACCRA Cost of Living Index
d. Ecotax

12. A real covenant is a legal obligation imposed in a deed by the seller upon the buyer of real estate to do or not to do something. Such restrictions frequently 'run with the land' and are enforceable on subsequent buyers of the property. In jurisdictions that use the Torrens system of land registration, _____ are generally registered against title.
a. Fraudulent trading
b. Feoffee
c. Bankruptcy in Canada
d. Restrictive covenants

13. To _____ is to impose a financial charge or other levy upon a taxpayer by a state or the functional equivalent of a state.

_____es are also imposed by many subnational entities. _____es consist of direct _____ or indirect _____, and may be paid in money or as its labour equivalent (often but not always unpaid.)

a. Tax
b. 130-30 fund
c. 100-year flood
d. 1921 recession

14. To tax is to impose a financial charge or other levy upon a taxpayer by a state or the functional equivalent of a state.

_____ are also imposed by many subnational entities. _____ consist of direct tax or indirect tax, and may be paid in money or as its labour equivalent (often but not always unpaid.)

   a. 130-30 fund
   b. 100-year flood
   c. 1921 recession
   d. Taxes

15. In economics, an _____ or spillover of an economic transaction is an impact on a party that is not directly involved in the transaction. In such a case, prices do not reflect the full costs or benefits in production or consumption of a product or service. A positive impact is called an external benefit, while a negative impact is called an external cost.
   a. Environmental impact assessment
   b. Existence value
   c. Environmental tariff
   d. Externality

16. A _____ is a situation that involves losing one quality or aspect of something in return for gaining another quality or aspect. It implies a decision to be made with full comprehension of both the upside and downside of a particular choice.

In economics the term is expressed as opportunity cost, referring the most preferred alternative given up.

   a. Nonmarket
   b. Trade-off
   c. Whitemail
   d. Friedman-Savage utility function

17. A _____ is a broad coalition government consisting of all parties (or all major parties) in the legislature, usually formed during a time of war or other national emergency.

During World War I the Conservative government of Sir Robert Borden invited the Liberal opposition to join the government as a means of dealing with the Conscription crisis of 1917. The Liberals, led by Sir Wilfrid Laurier refused; however, Borden was able to convince many individual Liberals to join what was called a Union Government, which defeated the Laurier Liberals in the fall 1917 election.

a. 100-year flood
b. 130-30 fund
c. National government
d. 1921 recession

18. _____ is an aspect of American jurisprudence under the Due Process Clause, involving substantive unenumerated rights. _____ is to be distinguished from procedural due process, which involves procedural unenumerated rights.

The term '_____', is commonly used in two ways: first to identify a particular line of cases, and second to signify a particular attitude toward judicial review under the Due Process Clause.

a. 100-year flood
b. 130-30 fund
c. 1921 recession
d. Substantive due process

19. The _____ consists of a number of economic theories which describe the nature of the firm, company including its existence, its behaviour, and its relationship with the market.

In simplified terms, the _____ aims to answer these questions:

1. Existence - why do firms emerge, why are not all transactions in the economy mediated over the market?
2. Boundaries - why the boundary between firms and the market is located exactly there? Which transactions are performed internally and which are negotiated on the market?
3. Organization - why are firms structured in such specific way? What is the interplay of formal and informal relationships?

Despite looking simple, these questions are not answered by the established economic theory, which usually views firms as given, and treats them as black boxes without any internal structure.

The First World War period saw a change of emphasis in economic theory away from industry-level analysis which mainly included analysing markets to analysis at the level of the firm, as it became increasingly clear that perfect competition was no longer an adequate model of how firms behaved. Economic theory till then had focussed on trying to understand markets alone and there had been little study on understanding why firms or organisations exist.

Chapter 9. Zoning and Growth Controls

a. Policy Ineffectiveness Proposition
b. Technology gap
c. Theory of the firm
d. Khazzoom-Brookes postulate

20. A _____ is a place of residence or refuge and comfort. It is usually a place in which an individual or a family can rest and be able to store personal property. Most modern-day households contain sanitary facilities and a means of preparing food.

 a. Home
 b. 100-year flood
 c. 1921 recession
 d. 130-30 fund

21. _____ is required to be paid by the Fifth Amendment to the U.S. Constitution (and counterpart state constitutions) when private property is taken (or in some states, damaged) for public use. For reasons of expedience, courts have been generally using fair market value as the measure of _____, reasoning that this is the amount that a willing seller would accept in a voluntary sales transaction and therefore it should also be payable in an involuntary one. However, the U.S. Supreme Court has repeatedly acknowledged that 'fair market value' as defined by it falls short of what sellers would demand and receive in voluntary transactions.

 a. Competition law theory
 b. Bona fide occupational qualification
 c. Clean Air Act Extension of 1970
 d. Just compensation

22. A municipality is an administrative entity composed of a clearly defined territory and its population and commonly denotes a city, town or a small grouping of them. A municipality is typically governed by a mayor and a city council or _____ council.

The notion of municipality includes townships but is not restricted to them.

 a. 130-30 fund
 b. 1921 recession
 c. 100-year flood
 d. Municipal

23. _____ is the a method of technical and economic research of the systems for purpose to optimize a parity between system's consumer functions or properties and expenses to achieve those functions or properties.

This methodology for continuous perfection of production, industrial technologies, organizational structures was developed by Juryj Sobolev in 1948 at the 'Perm telephone factory'

- 1948 Juryj Sobolev - the first success in application of a method analysis at the 'Perm telephone factory' .
- 1949 - the first application for the invention as result of use of the new method.

Today in economically developed countries practically each enterprise or the company use methodology of the kind of functional-cost analysis as a practice of the quality management, most full satisfying to principles of standards of series ISO 9000.

- Interest of consumer not in products itself, but the advantage which it will receive from its usage.
- The consumer aspires to reduce his expenses
- Functions needed by consumer can be executed in the various ways, and, hence, with various efficiency and expenses. Among possible alternatives of realization of functions exist such in which the parity of quality and the price is the optimal for the consumer.

The goal of _____ is achievement of the highest consumer satisfaction of production at simultaneous decrease in all kinds of industrial expenses Classical _____ has three English synonyms - Value Engineering, Value Management, Value Analysis.

a. Willingness to pay
b. Function cost analysis
c. Staple financing
d. Monopoly wage

24. _____ is a mechanism that allows people easily to buy and sell products. Services are often included in the scope of the term. _____ regulation is an economic term that describes restrictions in the market.

a. Financialization
b. Market dominance
c. Fixed exchange rate system
d. Product market

25. Economic _____ is defined as an excess distribution to any factor in a production process above that which is required to induce the factor into the process or any excess above that which is necessary to keep the factor in its current use..

Classical Factor _____ is primarily concerned with the fee paid for the use of fixed (e.g. natural) resources. The classical definition is expressed as any excess payment above that required to induce or provide for production.

a. 130-30 fund
b. 1921 recession
c. Rent
d. 100-year flood

26. _____ is a measurement of population per unit area or unit volume. It is frequently applied to living organisms, and particularly to humans. It is a key term used in geography.

a. 130-30 fund
b. Population density
c. 1921 recession
d. 100-year flood

27. In probability theory, a probability _____ of a random variable is a function which describes the density of probability at each point in the sample space. The probability of a random variable falling within a given set is given by the integral of its density over the set.

A probability _____ is most commonly associated with continuous univariate distributions.

a. Graphical model
b. Markov blanket
c. Density function
d. Memorylessness

28. _____ is the application of economic techniques to real estate markets. It tries to describe, explain, and predict patterns of prices, supply, and demand. The closely related fields of housing economics is narrower in scope, concentrating on residential real estate markets as does the research of real estate trends focus on the business and structural changes impacting the industry.

a. 1921 recession
b. 100-year flood
c. 130-30 fund
d. Real estate economics

29. Economics:

- _____, the desire to own something and the ability to pay for it
- _____ curve, a graphic representation of a _____ schedule
- _____ deposit, the money in checking accounts
- _____ pull theory, the theory that inflation occurs when _____ for goods and services exceeds existing supplies
- _____ schedule, a table that lists the quantity of a good a person will buy it each different price
- _____ side economics, the school of economics at believes government spending and tax cuts open economy by raising _____

a. Production
b. McKesson ' Robbins scandal
c. Variability
d. Demand

30. In economics, _____ is the ratio of the percent change in one variable to the percent change in another variable. It is a tool for measuring the responsiveness of a function to changes in parameters in a relative way. Commonly analyzed are _____ of substitution, price and wealth.
   a. ACEA agreement
   b. ACCRA Cost of Living Index
   c. Elasticity of demand
   d. Elasticity

31. Price _____ is defined as the measure of responsiveness in the quantity demanded for a commodity as a result of change in price of the same commodity. It is a measure of how consumers react to a change in price. In other words, it is percentage change in quantity demanded by the percentage change in price of the same commodity.
   a. Elasticity
   b. ACEA agreement
   c. ACCRA Cost of Living Index
   d. Elasticity of demand

32. Under the system of feudalism, a _____, fief, feud, feoff often consisted of inheritable lands or revenue-producing property granted by a liege lord, generally to a vassal, in return for a form of allegiance, originally to give him the means to fulfill his military duties when called upon. However anything of value could be held in fief, such as an office, a right of exploitation (e.g., hunting, fishing) or any other type of revenue, rather than the land it comes from.

Originally, the feudal institution of vassalage did not imply the giving or receiving of landholdings (which were granted only as a reward for loyalty), but by the eighth century the giving of a landholding was becoming standard.

a. 1921 recession
b. 130-30 fund
c. Fiefdom
d. 100-year flood

33. _____ in economics and business is the result of an exchange and from that trade we assign a numerical monetary value to a good, service or asset. If Alice trades Bob 4 apples for an orange, the _____ of an orange is 4 apples. Inversely, the _____ of an apple is 1/4 oranges.
a. Price war
b. Price
c. Price book
d. Premium pricing

Chapter 10. Externalities from Autos

1. _____ is the removal or simplification of government rules and regulations that constrain the operation of market forces. _____ does not mean elimination of laws against fraud, but eliminating or reducing government control of how business is done, thereby moving toward a more free market.

The stated rationale for '_____' is often that fewer and simpler regulations will lead to a raised level of competitiveness, therefore higher productivity, more efficiency and lower prices overall.

   a. Secular basis
   b. Fundamental psychological law
   c. Macroeconomic policy instruments
   d. Deregulation

2. A _____ is a bond which is worth a certain monetary value and which may only be spent for specific reasons or on specific goods. Examples include -- but are not limited to -- housing, travel and food _____s. The term _____ is also a synonym for receipt, and is often used to refer to receipts used as evidence of, for example, the declaration that a service has been performed or that an expenditure has been made.
   a. 130-30 fund
   b. 1921 recession
   c. 100-year flood
   d. Voucher

3. A _____ is the procedure of systematically acquiring and recording information about the members of a given population. It is a regularly occurring and official count of a particular population. The term is used mostly in connection with national 'population and door to door _____es' (to be taken every 10 years according to United Nations recommendations), agriculture, and business _____es.
   a. 130-30 fund
   b. 100-year flood
   c. 1921 recession
   d. Census

4. In economics, an _____ or spillover of an economic transaction is an impact on a party that is not directly involved in the transaction. In such a case, prices do not reflect the full costs or benefits in production or consumption of a product or service. A positive impact is called an external benefit, while a negative impact is called an external cost.
   a. Externality
   b. Environmental tariff
   c. Environmental impact assessment
   d. Existence value

Chapter 10. Externalities from Autos 73

5. The term '_____' refers to the concept of collecting information and attempting to spot a pattern in the information. In some fields of study, the term '_____' has more formally-defined meanings.

In project management _____ is a mathematical technique that uses historical results to predict future outcome.

   a. Trend analysis
   b. Quantile regression
   c. Probit model
   d. Coefficient of determination

6. _____ is an ad valorem tax that an owner is required to pay on the value of the property being taxed. _____ can be defined as 'generally, tax imposed by municipalities upon owners of property within their jurisdiction based on the value of such property.' There are three species or types of property: Land, Improvements to Land (immovable manmade objects; i.e., buildings), and Personal (movable manmade objects.) Real estate, real property or realty are all terms for the combination of land and improvements.
   a. Chief Financial Officers Act of 1990
   b. Property tax
   c. Bank regulation
   d. Community property

7. Economics:

   - _____,the desire to own something and the ability to pay for it
   - _____ curve,a graphic representation of a _____ schedule
   - _____ deposit, the money in checking accounts
   - _____ pull theory,the theory that inflation occurs when _____ for goods and services exceeds existing supplies
   - _____ schedule,a table that lists the quantity of a good a person will buy it each different price
   - _____ side economics,the school of economics at believes government spending and tax cuts open economy by raising _____

   a. Variability
   b. Production
   c. McKesson ' Robbins scandal
   d. Demand

8. To _____ is to impose a financial charge or other levy upon a taxpayer by a state or the functional equivalent of a state.

_____es are also imposed by many subnational entities. _____es consist of direct _____ or indirect _____, and may be paid in money or as its labour equivalent (often but not always unpaid.)

a. 130-30 fund
b. 1921 recession
c. 100-year flood
d. Tax

9. To tax is to impose a financial charge or other levy upon a taxpayer by a state or the functional equivalent of a state.

_____ are also imposed by many subnational entities. _____ consist of direct tax or indirect tax, and may be paid in money or as its labour equivalent (often but not always unpaid.)

a. 1921 recession
b. 100-year flood
c. 130-30 fund
d. Taxes

10. An _____ is a tax levied on the financial income of people, corporations, or other legal entities. Various _____ systems exist, with varying degrees of tax incidence. Income taxation can be progressive, proportional, or regressive.

a. Income tax
b. ACEA agreement
c. ACCRA Cost of Living Index
d. AD-IA Model

11. In economics _____ is defined as the sum of private and external costs. Economic theorists ascribe individual decision-making to a calculation costs and benefits. Rational choice theory assumes that individuals only consider their own private costs when making decisions, not the costs that may be borne by others.

a. Social cost
b. Cost-Volume-Profit Analysis
c. Khozraschyot
d. Psychic cost

12. In the study of human settlements, an _____ is an extended city or town area comprising the built-up area of a central place (usually a municipality) and any suburbs linked by continuous urban area. In France, INSEE the French Statistical Institute, translate it as 'Unité urbaine' which means continuous urbanized area. However, because of differences in definitions of what does and does not constitute an '_____', as well as variations and limitations in statistical or geographical methodology, it can be problematic to compare different _____s around the world.
   a. ACCRA Cost of Living Index
   b. AD-IA Model
   c. Agglomeration
   d. ACEA agreement

13. _____s is the social science that studies the production, distribution, and consumption of goods and services. The term _____s comes from the Ancient Greek οἰκονομία from οἶκος (oikos, 'house') + νόμος (nomos, 'custom' or 'law'), hence 'rules of the house(hold)'. Current _____ models developed out of the broader field of political economy in the late 19th century, owing to a desire to use an empirical approach more akin to the physical sciences.
   a. Economic
   b. Opportunity cost
   c. Energy economics
   d. Inflation

14. In economics, a _____ is a graph of the costs of production as a function of total quantity produced. In a free market economy, productively efficient firms use these curves to find the optimal point of production, where they make the most profits. There are a few different types of _____s, each relevant to a different area of economics.
   a. Demand curve
   b. Cost curve
   c. Phillips curve
   d. Kuznets curve

15. Under the system of feudalism, a _____, fief, feud, feoff often consisted of inheritable lands or revenue-producing property granted by a liege lord, generally to a vassal, in return for a form of allegiance, originally to give him the means to fulfill his military duties when called upon. However anything of value could be held in fief, such as an office, a right of exploitation (e.g., hunting, fishing) or any other type of revenue, rather than the land it comes from.

Originally, the feudal institution of vassalage did not imply the giving or receiving of landholdings (which were granted only as a reward for loyalty), but by the eighth century the giving of a landholding was becoming standard.

a. 1921 recession
b. 130-30 fund
c. 100-year flood
d. Fiefdom

16. _____ is a set of properties and characteristics of the environment, either generalized or local, as they impinge on human beings and other organisms.

_____ is a general term which can refer to varied characteristics that relate to the natural environment as well as the built environment, such as air and water purity or pollution, noise and the potential effects which such characteristics may have on physical and mental health caused by human activities.

In the USA the term is applied with a body of federal and state standards and regulations that are monitored by regulatory agencies.

a. ACEA agreement
b. AD-IA Model
c. ACCRA Cost of Living Index
d. Environmental quality

17. _____, in law and economics, is a form of risk management primarily used to hedge against the risk of a contingent loss. _____ is defined as the equitable transfer of the risk of a loss, from one entity to another, in exchange for a premium, and can be thought of as a guaranteed small loss to prevent a large, possibly devastating loss. An insurer is a company selling the _____; an insured or policyholder is the person or entity buying the _____.

a. ACEA agreement
b. ACCRA Cost of Living Index
c. AD-IA Model
d. Insurance

18. _____ is the shortage of common things such as food, clothing, shelter and safe drinking water, all of which determine the quality of life. It may also include the lack of access to opportunities such as education and employment which aid the escape from _____ and/or allow one to enjoy the respect of fellow citizens. According to Mollie Orshansky who developed the _____ measurements used by the U.S. government, 'to be poor is to be deprived of those goods and services and pleasures which others around us take for granted.' Ongoing debates over causes, effects and best ways to measure _____, directly influence the design and implementation of _____-reduction programs and are therefore relevant to the fields of public administration and international development.

Chapter 10. Externalities from Autos 77

a. Growth Elasticity of Poverty
b. Liberal welfare reforms
c. Poverty map
d. Poverty

19. _____ is a form of housing tenure in which the property is owned by a government authority, which may be central or local. Social housing is an umbrella term referring to rental housing which may be owned and managed by the state, by not-for-profit organizations, or by a combination of the two, usually with the aim of providing affordable housing.

Although the common goal of _____ is to provide affordable housing, the details, terminology, definitions of poverty and other criteria for allocation vary.

a. 1921 recession
b. Public housing
c. 100-year flood
d. 130-30 fund

20. The _____ is 'the basic residential unit in which economic production, consumption, inheritance, child rearing, and shelter are organized and carried out'; [the _____] 'may or may not be synonymous with family'.

The _____ is the basic unit of analysis in many social, microeconomic and government models. The term refers to all individuals who live in the same dwelling.

a. 130-30 fund
b. Household
c. Family economics
d. 100-year flood

21. _____ was a survey conducted by the U.S. Department of Justice to gauge the prevalence of alcohol and illegal drug use among prior arrestees. It was a reformulation of the prior Drug Use Forecasting (DUF) program, focused on five drugs in particular: cocaine, marijuana, methamphetamine, opiates, and PCP.

Participants were randomly selected from arrest records in major metropolitan areas; because no personally identifying information is taken from each record chosen, the resulting data can be correlated to arrest rates, but not to the total population of persons charged.

a. AD-IA Model
b. Arrestee Drug Abuse Monitoring
c. ACCRA Cost of Living Index
d. ACEA agreement

Chapter 11. Mass Transit

1. _____ is the removal or simplification of government rules and regulations that constrain the operation of market forces. _____ does not mean elimination of laws against fraud, but eliminating or reducing government control of how business is done, thereby moving toward a more free market.

The stated rationale for '_____' is often that fewer and simpler regulations will lead to a raised level of competitiveness, therefore higher productivity, more efficiency and lower prices overall.

   a. Deregulation
   b. Secular basis
   c. Macroeconomic policy instruments
   d. Fundamental psychological law

2. A _____ is the procedure of systematically acquiring and recording information about the members of a given population. It is a regularly occurring and official count of a particular population. The term is used mostly in connection with national 'population and door to door _____es' (to be taken every 10 years according to United Nations recommendations), agriculture, and business _____es.
   a. 100-year flood
   b. 1921 recession
   c. 130-30 fund
   d. Census

3. A _____ is a bond which is worth a certain monetary value and which may only be spent for specific reasons or on specific goods. Examples include -- but are not limited to -- housing, travel and food _____s. The term _____ is also a synonym for receipt, and is often used to refer to receipts used as evidence of, for example, the declaration that a service has been performed or that an expenditure has been made.
   a. 100-year flood
   b. 130-30 fund
   c. 1921 recession
   d. Voucher

4. _____ is the shortage of common things such as food, clothing, shelter and safe drinking water, all of which determine the quality of life. It may also include the lack of access to opportunities such as education and employment which aid the escape from _____ and/or allow one to enjoy the respect of fellow citizens. According to Mollie Orshansky who developed the _____ measurements used by the U.S. government, 'to be poor is to be deprived of those goods and services and pleasures which others around us take for granted.' Ongoing debates over causes, effects and best ways to measure _____, directly influence the design and implementation of _____-reduction programs and are therefore relevant to the fields of public administration and international development.

a. Poverty map
b. Growth Elasticity of Poverty
c. Liberal welfare reforms
d. Poverty

5. _____ is a form of housing tenure in which the property is owned by a government authority, which may be central or local. Social housing is an umbrella term referring to rental housing which may be owned and managed by the state, by not-for-profit organizations, or by a combination of the two, usually with the aim of providing affordable housing.

Although the common goal of _____ is to provide affordable housing, the details, terminology, definitions of poverty and other criteria for allocation vary.

a. 100-year flood
b. 1921 recession
c. Public housing
d. 130-30 fund

6. The _____ is 'the basic residential unit in which economic production, consumption, inheritance, child rearing, and shelter are organized and carried out'; [the _____] 'may or may not be synonomous with family'.

The _____ is the basic unit of analysis in many social, microeconomic and government models. The term refers to all individuals who live in the same dwelling.

a. Family economics
b. 100-year flood
c. 130-30 fund
d. Household

7. _____ in economics and business is the result of an exchange and from that trade we assign a numerical monetary value to a good, service or asset. If Alice trades Bob 4 apples for an orange, the _____ of an orange is 4 apples. Inversely, the _____ of an apple is 1/4 oranges.
a. Price war
b. Price book
c. Premium pricing
d. Price

8. _____ is the a method of technical and economic research of the systems for purpose to optimize a parity between system's consumer functions or properties and expenses to achieve those functions or properties.

Chapter 11. Mass Transit

This methodology for continuous perfection of production, industrial technologies, organizational structures was developed by Juryj Sobolev in 1948 at the 'Perm telephone factory'

- 1948 Juryj Sobolev - the first success in application of a method analysis at the 'Perm telephone factory'.
- 1949 - the first application for the invention as result of use of the new method.

Today in economically developed countries practically each enterprise or the company use methodology of the kind of functional-cost analysis as a practice of the quality management, most full satisfying to principles of standards of series ISO 9000.

- Interest of consumer not in products itself, but the advantage which it will receive from its usage.
- The consumer aspires to reduce his expenses
- Functions needed by consumer can be executed in the various ways, and, hence, with various efficiency and expenses. Among possible alternatives of realization of functions exist such in which the parity of quality and the price is the optimal for the consumer.

The goal of _____ is achievement of the highest consumer satisfaction of production at simultaneous decrease in all kinds of industrial expenses Classical _____ has three English synonyms - Value Engineering, Value Management, Value Analysis.

a. Monopoly wage
b. Staple financing
c. Willingness to pay
d. Function cost analysis

9. Economics:

   - _____,the desire to own something and the ability to pay for it
   - _____ curve,a graphic representation of a _____ schedule
   - _____ deposit, the money in checking accounts
   - _____ pull theory,the theory that inflation occurs when _____ for goods and services exceeds existing supplies
   - _____ schedule,a table that lists the quantity of a good a person will buy it each different price
   - _____ side economics,the school of economics at believes government spending and tax cuts open economy by raising _____

a. McKesson ' Robbins scandal
b. Production
c. Variability
d. Demand

10. In economics, _____ is the ratio of the percent change in one variable to the percent change in another variable. It is a tool for measuring the responsiveness of a function to changes in parameters in a relative way. Commonly analyzed are _____ of substitution, price and wealth.
   a. Elasticity
   b. ACEA agreement
   c. ACCRA Cost of Living Index
   d. Elasticity of demand

11. _____ is a broad label that refers to any individuals or households that use goods and services generated within the economy. The concept of a _____ is used in different contexts, so that the usage and significance of the term may vary.

Typically when business people and economists talk of _____s they are talking about person as _____, an aggregated commodity item with little individuality other than that expressed in the buy/not-buy decision.

   a. 1921 recession
   b. 100-year flood
   c. 130-30 fund
   d. Consumer

12. _____ is a measurement of population per unit area or unit volume. It is frequently applied to living organisms, and particularly to humans. It is a key term used in geography.
   a. 1921 recession
   b. 130-30 fund
   c. 100-year flood
   d. Population density

13. _____ is an ad valorem tax that an owner is required to pay on the value of the property being taxed. _____ can be defined as 'generally, tax imposed by municipalities upon owners of property within their jurisdiction based on the value of such property.' There are three species or types of property: Land, Improvements to Land (immovable manmade objects; i.e., buildings), and Personal (movable manmade objects.) Real estate, real property or realty are all terms for the combination of land and improvements.

a. Community property
b. Chief Financial Officers Act of 1990
c. Bank regulation
d. Property tax

14. In probability theory, a probability _____ of a random variable is a function which describes the density of probability at each point in the sample space. The probability of a random variable falling within a given set is given by the integral of its density over the set.

A probability _____ is most commonly associated with continuous univariate distributions.

a. Graphical model
b. Markov blanket
c. Density function
d. Memorylessness

15. _____s are a type of administrative division, in some countries managed by a local government. They vary greatly in size, spanning entire regions or counties, several municipalities, or subdivisions of municipalities.

In Austria, a _____ or Bezirk is an administrative division normally encompassing several municipalities, roughly equivalent to the Landkreis in Germany.

a. 1921 recession
b. 130-30 fund
c. 100-year flood
d. District

16. To _____ is to impose a financial charge or other levy upon a taxpayer by a state or the functional equivalent of a state.

_____es are also imposed by many subnational entities. _____es consist of direct _____ or indirect _____, and may be paid in money or as its labour equivalent (often but not always unpaid.)

a. 100-year flood
b. 130-30 fund
c. 1921 recession
d. Tax

17. To tax is to impose a financial charge or other levy upon a taxpayer by a state or the functional equivalent of a state.

_____ are also imposed by many subnational entities. _____ consist of direct tax or indirect tax, and may be paid in money or as its labour equivalent (often but not always unpaid.)

   a. 130-30 fund
   b. 100-year flood
   c. 1921 recession
   d. Taxes

18. A _____ is a situation that involves losing one quality or aspect of something in return for gaining another quality or aspect. It implies a decision to be made with full comprehension of both the upside and downside of a particular choice.

In economics the term is expressed as opportunity cost, referring the most preferred alternative given up.

   a. Whitemail
   b. Friedman-Savage utility function
   c. Nonmarket
   d. Trade-off

19. _____, in microeconomics, are the cost advantages that a business obtains due to expansion. They are factors that cause a producere;s average cost per unit to fall as scale is increased. _____ is a long run concept and refers to reductions in unit cost as the size of a facility, or scale, increases.
   a. Isoquant
   b. Underinvestment employment relationship
   c. Economic production quantity
   d. Economies of scale

20. _____ is the incidence or process of transferring ownership of a business, enterprise, agency or public service from the public sector (government) to the private sector (business.) In a broader sense, _____ refers to transfer of any government function to the private sector including governmental functions like revenue collection and law enforcement.

The term '_____' also has been used to describe two unrelated transactions.

   a. Performance reports
   b. Compound empowerment
   c. Ricardian equivalence
   d. Privatization

21. In microeconomics, _____ is quite simply the conversion of inputs into outputs. It is an economic process that uses resources to create a good or service that is suitable for exchange. This can include manufacturing, storing, shipping, and packaging.
   a. Solved
   b. Red Guards
   c. MET
   d. Production

22. _____ in economics refers to metrics and measures of output from production processes, per unit of input. Labor _____, for example, is typically measured as a ratio of output per labor-hour, an input. _____ may be conceived of as a metrics of the technical or engineering efficiency of production.
   a. Production-possibility frontier
   b. Fordism
   c. Piece work
   d. Productivity

23. _____ is the process by which the activities of an organization, particularly those regarding decision-making, become concentrated within a particular location and/or group.

In political science, this refers to the concentration of a government's power - both geographically and politically, into a centralized government.

   a. Centralization
   b. Microcap stock
   c. Product innovation
   d. Teaser rate

24. _____ is the physical growth of rural or natural land into urban areas as a result of population immigration to an existing urban area. Effects include change in density and administration services. While the exact definition and population size of urbanized areas varies among different countries, _____ is attributed to growth of cities.
   a. Urban renewal
   b. Urbanization
   c. ACCRA Cost of Living Index
   d. Urban prairie

25. _____ is a term used to describe the process of population movement from within towns and cities to the rural-urban fringe. It is one of the many causes of the increase in urban sprawl. Many residents of metropolitan areas no longer live and work within the central urban area, choosing instead to live in satellite communities called suburbs and commute to work via automobile or mass transit.
   a. Rural exodus
   b. Redevelopment
   c. 100-year flood
   d. Suburbanization

Chapter 12. Crime 87

1. _____ is the shortage of common things such as food, clothing, shelter and safe drinking water, all of which determine the quality of life. It may also include the lack of access to opportunities such as education and employment which aid the escape from _____ and/or allow one to enjoy the respect of fellow citizens. According to Mollie Orshansky who developed the _____ measurements used by the U.S. government, 'to be poor is to be deprived of those goods and services and pleasures which others around us take for granted.' Ongoing debates over causes, effects and best ways to measure _____, directly influence the design and implementation of _____-reduction programs and are therefore relevant to the fields of public administration and international development.
    a. Poverty
    b. Growth Elasticity of Poverty
    c. Poverty map
    d. Liberal welfare reforms

2. _____ is a category of crime that includes, among other crimes, burglary, larceny, theft, motor vehicle theft, arson, shoplifting, and vandalism. _____ only involves the taking of money or property, and does not involve force or threat of force against a victim. Although robbery involves taking property, it is classified as a violent crime, as force or threat of force on an individual that is present is involved in contrast to burglary which is typically of an unoccupied dwelling or other unoccupied building.
    a. 100-year flood
    b. Property crime
    c. 1921 recession
    d. 130-30 fund

3. _____ has several particular meanings:

    - in mathematics
        - _____ function
        - Euler _____
        - _____
        - _____ subgroup
        - method of _____s (partial differential equations)
    - in physics and engineering
        - any _____ curve that shows the relationship between certain input- and output parameters, e.g.
        - an I-V or current-voltage _____ is the current in a circuit as a function of the applied voltage
        - Receiver-Operator _____
    - in fiction
        - in Dungeons ' Dragons, _____ is another name for ability score

a. Demand
b. Technocracy
c. Russian financial crisis
d. Characteristic

4. _____s are a type of administrative division, in some countries managed by a local government. They vary greatly in size, spanning entire regions or counties, several municipalities, or subdivisions of municipalities.

In Austria, a _____ or Bezirk is an administrative division normally encompassing several municipalities, roughly equivalent to the Landkreis in Germany.

a. 130-30 fund
b. 100-year flood
c. 1921 recession
d. District

5. The _____ is 'the basic residential unit in which economic production, consumption, inheritance, child rearing, and shelter are organized and carried out'; [the _____] 'may or may not be synonomous with family'.

The _____ is the basic unit of analysis in many social, microeconomic and government models. The term refers to all individuals who live in the same dwelling.

a. 100-year flood
b. 130-30 fund
c. Family economics
d. Household

6. _____s is the social science that studies the production, distribution, and consumption of goods and services. The term _____s comes from the Ancient Greek οἰκονομία from οἶκος (oikos, 'house') + νόμος (nomos, 'custom' or 'law'), hence 'rules of the house(hold)'. Current _____ models developed out of the broader field of political economy in the late 19th century, owing to a desire to use an empirical approach more akin to the physical sciences.

a. Inflation
b. Energy economics
c. Opportunity cost
d. Economic

7. In economics, game theory, and decision theory the _____ theorem or _____ hypothesis predicts that the 'betting preferences' of people with regard to uncertain outcomes (gambles) can be described by a mathematical relation which takes into account the size of a payout (whether in money or other goods), the probability of occurrence, risk aversion, and the different utility of the same payout to people with different assets or personal preferences. It is a more sophisticated theory than simply predicting that choices will be made based on expected value (which takes into account only the size of the payout and the probability of occurrence.)

Daniel Bernoulli described the complete theory in 1738.

  a. Utility
  b. Expected utility hypothesis
  c. Ordinal utility
  d. Expected utility

8. In economics, _____ is a measure of the relative satisfaction from consumption of various goods and services. Given this measure, one may speak meaningfully of increasing or decreasing _____, and thereby explain economic behavior in terms of attempts to increase one's _____. For illustrative purposes, changes in _____ are sometimes expressed in units called utils.
  a. Expected utility hypothesis
  b. Ordinal utility
  c. Utility
  d. Utility function

9. _____ can be generally defined as the course of action or inaction taken by governmental entities with regard to a particular issue or set of issues. Other scholars define it as a system of 'courses of action, regulatory measures, laws, and funding priorities concerning a given topic promulgated by a governmental entity or its representatives.' _____ is commonly embodied 'in constitutions, legislative acts, and judicial decisions.'

In the United States, this concept refers not only to the end result of policies, but more broadly to the decision-making and analysis of governmental decisions. _____ is also considered an academic discipline, as it is studied by professors and students at _____ schools of major universities throughout the country.

  a. 1921 recession
  b. Public policy
  c. 100-year flood
  d. 130-30 fund

10. _____ refers to the stock of skills and knowledge embodied in the ability to perform labor so as to produce economic value. It is the skills and knowledge gained by a worker through education and experience. Many early economic theories refer to it simply as labor, one of three factors of production, and consider it to be a fungible resource -- homogeneous and easily interchangeable. Other conceptions of labor dispense with these assumptions.

 a. Human capital
 b. Price theory
 c. General equilibrium
 d. Law of increasing costs

11. In the study of human settlements, an _____ is an extended city or town area comprising the built-up area of a central place (usually a municipality) and any suburbs linked by continuous urban area. In France, INSEE the French Statistical Institute, translate it as 'Unité urbaine' which means continuous urbanized area. However, because of differences in definitions of what does and does not constitute an '_____', as well as variations and limitations in statistical or geographical methodology, it can be problematic to compare different _____s around the world.

 a. ACEA agreement
 b. ACCRA Cost of Living Index
 c. AD-IA Model
 d. Agglomeration

Chapter 13. Why Is Housing Different? 91

1. _____ is the application of economic techniques to real estate markets. It tries to describe, explain, and predict patterns of prices, supply, and demand. The closely related fields of housing economics is narrower in scope, concentrating on residential real estate markets as does the research of real estate trends focus on the business and structural changes impacting the industry.
    a. 100-year flood
    b. 130-30 fund
    c. Real estate economics
    d. 1921 recession

2. _____ is a mechanism that allows people easily to buy and sell products. Services are often included in the scope of the term. _____ regulation is an economic term that describes restrictions in the market.
    a. Financialization
    b. Fixed exchange rate system
    c. Market dominance
    d. Product market

3. Economics:

    - _____,the desire to own something and the ability to pay for it
    - _____ curve,a graphic representation of a _____ schedule
    - _____ deposit, the money in checking accounts
    - _____ pull theory,the theory that inflation occurs when _____ for goods and services exceeds existing supplies
    - _____ schedule,a table that lists the quantity of a good a person will buy it each different price
    - _____ side economics,the school of economics at believes government spending and tax cuts open economy by raising _____

    a. McKesson ' Robbins scandal
    b. Demand
    c. Variability
    d. Production

4. In economics, _____ is the ratio of the percent change in one variable to the percent change in another variable. It is a tool for measuring the responsiveness of a function to changes in parameters in a relative way. Commonly analyzed are _____ of substitution, price and wealth.

Chapter 13. Why Is Housing Different?

a. ACEA agreement
b. ACCRA Cost of Living Index
c. Elasticity of demand
d. Elasticity

5. Price _____ is defined as the measure of responsiveness in the quantity demanded for a commodity as a result of change in price of the same commodity. It is a measure of how consumers react to a change in price. In other words, it is percentage change in quantity demanded by the percentage change in price of the same commodity.
   a. Elasticity
   b. ACCRA Cost of Living Index
   c. Elasticity of demand
   d. ACEA agreement

6. _____ in economics and business is the result of an exchange and from that trade we assign a numerical monetary value to a good, service or asset. If Alice trades Bob 4 apples for an orange, the _____ of an orange is 4 apples. Inversely, the _____ of an apple is 1/4 oranges.
   a. Price
   b. Premium pricing
   c. Price book
   d. Price war

7. _____ is an ad valorem tax that an owner is required to pay on the value of the property being taxed. _____ can be defined as 'generally, tax imposed by municipalities upon owners of property within their jurisdiction based on the value of such property.' There are three species or types of property: Land, Improvements to Land (immovable manmade objects; i.e., buildings), and Personal (movable manmade objects.) Real estate, real property or realty are all terms for the combination of land and improvements.
   a. Bank regulation
   b. Chief Financial Officers Act of 1990
   c. Community property
   d. Property tax

8. _____ can be generally defined as the course of action or inaction taken by governmental entities with regard to a particular issue or set of issues. Other scholars define it as a system of 'courses of action, regulatory measures, laws, and funding priorities concerning a given topic promulgated by a governmental entity or its representatives.' _____ is commonly embodied 'in constitutions, legislative acts, and judicial decisions.'

Chapter 13. Why Is Housing Different?

In the United States, this concept refers not only to the end result of policies, but more broadly to the decision-making and analysis of governmental decisions. _____ is also considered an academic discipline, as it is studied by professors and students at _____ schools of major universities throughout the country.

a. Public policy
b. 1921 recession
c. 100-year flood
d. 130-30 fund

9. To _____ is to impose a financial charge or other levy upon a taxpayer by a state or the functional equivalent of a state.

_____es are also imposed by many subnational entities. _____es consist of direct _____ or indirect _____, and may be paid in money or as its labour equivalent (often but not always unpaid.)

a. 100-year flood
b. 130-30 fund
c. Tax
d. 1921 recession

10. To tax is to impose a financial charge or other levy upon a taxpayer by a state or the functional equivalent of a state.

_____ are also imposed by many subnational entities. _____ consist of direct tax or indirect tax, and may be paid in money or as its labour equivalent (often but not always unpaid.)

a. 1921 recession
b. 130-30 fund
c. 100-year flood
d. Taxes

11. _____ is the shortage of common things such as food, clothing, shelter and safe drinking water, all of which determine the quality of life. It may also include the lack of access to opportunities such as education and employment which aid the escape from _____ and/or allow one to enjoy the respect of fellow citizens. According to Mollie Orshansky who developed the _____ measurements used by the U.S. government, 'to be poor is to be deprived of those goods and services and pleasures which others around us take for granted.' Ongoing debates over causes, effects and best ways to measure _____, directly influence the design and implementation of _____-reduction programs and are therefore relevant to the fields of public administration and international development.

a. Liberal welfare reforms
b. Growth Elasticity of Poverty
c. Poverty
d. Poverty map

12. _____s are a type of administrative division, in some countries managed by a local government. They vary greatly in size, spanning entire regions or counties, several municipalities, or subdivisions of municipalities.

In Austria, a _____ or Bezirk is an administrative division normally encompassing several municipalities, roughly equivalent to the Landkreis in Germany.

a. District
b. 1921 recession
c. 100-year flood
d. 130-30 fund

13. The _____ is 'the basic residential unit in which economic production, consumption, inheritance, child rearing, and shelter are organized and carried out'; [the _____] 'may or may not be synonomous with family'.

The _____ is the basic unit of analysis in many social, microeconomic and government models. The term refers to all individuals who live in the same dwelling.

a. 100-year flood
b. Family economics
c. 130-30 fund
d. Household

Chapter 14. Housing Policy

1. _____ is a form of housing tenure in which the property is owned by a government authority, which may be central or local. Social housing is an umbrella term referring to rental housing which may be owned and managed by the state, by not-for-profit organizations, or by a combination of the two, usually with the aim of providing affordable housing.

Although the common goal of _____ is to provide affordable housing, the details, terminology, definitions of poverty and other criteria for allocation vary.

   a. 1921 recession
   b. 130-30 fund
   c. Public housing
   d. 100-year flood

2. _____ is a broad label that refers to any individuals or households that use goods and services generated within the economy. The concept of a _____ is used in different contexts, so that the usage and significance of the term may vary.

Typically when business people and economists talk of _____s they are talking about person as _____, an aggregated commodity item with little individuality other than that expressed in the buy/not-buy decision.

   a. 100-year flood
   b. 130-30 fund
   c. 1921 recession
   d. Consumer

3. _____ is the shortage of common things such as food, clothing, shelter and safe drinking water, all of which determine the quality of life. It may also include the lack of access to opportunities such as education and employment which aid the escape from _____ and/or allow one to enjoy the respect of fellow citizens. According to Mollie Orshansky who developed the _____ measurements used by the U.S. government, 'to be poor is to be deprived of those goods and services and pleasures which others around us take for granted.' Ongoing debates over causes, effects and best ways to measure _____, directly influence the design and implementation of _____-reduction programs and are therefore relevant to the fields of public administration and international development.
   a. Poverty map
   b. Growth Elasticity of Poverty
   c. Liberal welfare reforms
   d. Poverty

4. _____ is a mechanism that allows people easily to buy and sell products. Services are often included in the scope of the term. _____ regulation is an economic term that describes restrictions in the market.

a. Financialization
b. Fixed exchange rate system
c. Market dominance
d. Product market

5. _____s are a type of administrative division, in some countries managed by a local government. They vary greatly in size, spanning entire regions or counties, several municipalities, or subdivisions of municipalities.

In Austria, a _____ or Bezirk is an administrative division normally encompassing several municipalities, roughly equivalent to the Landkreis in Germany.

a. 1921 recession
b. District
c. 100-year flood
d. 130-30 fund

6. The _____ is 'the basic residential unit in which economic production, consumption, inheritance, child rearing, and shelter are organized and carried out'; [the _____] 'may or may not be synonomous with family'.

The _____ is the basic unit of analysis in many social, microeconomic and government models. The term refers to all individuals who live in the same dwelling.

a. 100-year flood
b. Family economics
c. 130-30 fund
d. Household

7. _____ in economics and business is the result of an exchange and from that trade we assign a numerical monetary value to a good, service or asset. If Alice trades Bob 4 apples for an orange, the _____ of an orange is 4 apples. Inversely, the _____ of an apple is 1/4 oranges.
a. Price
b. Premium pricing
c. Price book
d. Price war

8. _____ is the incidence or process of transferring ownership of a business, enterprise, agency or public service from the public sector (government) to the private sector (business.) In a broader sense, _____ refers to transfer of any government function to the private sector including governmental functions like revenue collection and law enforcement.

The term '_____' also has been used to describe two unrelated transactions.

a. Ricardian equivalence
b. Performance reports
c. Compound empowerment
d. Privatization

9. _____ is the application of economic techniques to real estate markets. It tries to describe, explain, and predict patterns of prices, supply, and demand. The closely related fields of housing economics is narrower in scope, concentrating on residential real estate markets as does the research of real estate trends focus on the business and structural changes impacting the industry.

a. 1921 recession
b. 130-30 fund
c. 100-year flood
d. Real estate economics

10. Economic _____ is defined as an excess distribution to any factor in a production process above that which is required to induce the factor into the process or any excess above that which is necessary to keep the factor in its current use..

Classical Factor _____ is primarily concerned with the fee paid for the use of fixed (e.g. natural) resources. The classical definition is expressed as any excess payment above that required to induce or provide for production.

a. 1921 recession
b. 130-30 fund
c. 100-year flood
d. Rent

11. The _____ is a Cabinet-level office, and is the largest office within the Executive Office of the President of the United States (EOP.) It is an important conduit by which the White House oversees the activities of federal agencies. OMB is tasked with giving expert advice to senior White House officials on a range of topics relating to federal policy, management, legislative, regulatory, and budgetary issues.

a. ACEA agreement
b. ACCRA Cost of Living Index
c. Office of Management and Budget
d. AD-IA Model

12. _____ is an ad valorem tax that an owner is required to pay on the value of the property being taxed. _____ can be defined as 'generally, tax imposed by municipalities upon owners of property within their jurisdiction based on the value of such property.' There are three species or types of property: Land, Improvements to Land (immovable manmade objects; i.e., buildings), and Personal (movable manmade objects.) Real estate, real property or realty are all terms for the combination of land and improvements.

   a. Chief Financial Officers Act of 1990
   b. Community property
   c. Bank regulation
   d. Property tax

13. To _____ is to impose a financial charge or other levy upon a taxpayer by a state or the functional equivalent of a state.

   _____es are also imposed by many subnational entities. _____es consist of direct _____ or indirect _____, and may be paid in money or as its labour equivalent (often but not always unpaid.)

   a. 100-year flood
   b. 1921 recession
   c. 130-30 fund
   d. Tax

14. _____ is the process of changing the way taxes are collected or managed by the government.

   _____ers have different goals. Some seek to reduce the level of taxation of all people by the government.

   a. Special-purpose local-option sales tax
   b. Tax Reform
   c. Tax break
   d. Nil-rate band

15. A _____ refers to any type debt instrument, such as a loan, bond, mortgage that does not have a fixed rate of interest over the life of the instrument. Such debt typically uses an index or other base rate for establishing the interest rate for each relevant period. One of the most common rates to use as the basis for applying interest rates is the London Inter-bank Offered Rate, or LIBOR

   a. Disposal tax effect
   b. Moneylender
   c. Floating interest rate
   d. Money market

Chapter 14. Housing Policy

16. Economics:

    - _____, the desire to own something and the ability to pay for it
    - _____ curve, a graphic representation of a _____ schedule
    - _____ deposit, the money in checking accounts
    - _____ pull theory, the theory that inflation occurs when _____ for goods and services exceeds existing supplies
    - _____ schedule, a table that lists the quantity of a good a person will buy it each different price
    - _____ side economics, the school of economics at believes government spending and tax cuts open economy by raising _____

    a. Production
    b. Variability
    c. McKesson ' Robbins scandal
    d. Demand

17. In economics, _____ is the ratio of the percent change in one variable to the percent change in another variable. It is a tool for measuring the responsiveness of a function to changes in parameters in a relative way. Commonly analyzed are _____ of substitution, price and wealth.
    a. ACEA agreement
    b. ACCRA Cost of Living Index
    c. Elasticity of demand
    d. Elasticity

18. Price _____ is defined as the measure of responsiveness in the quantity demanded for a commodity as a result of change in price of the same commodity. It is a measure of how consumers react to a change in price. In other words, it is percentage change in quantity demanded by the percentage change in price of the same commodity.
    a. Elasticity
    b. ACCRA Cost of Living Index
    c. Elasticity of demand
    d. ACEA agreement

19. The _____ is a tax credit created under the Tax Reform Act of 1986 that gives incentives for the utilization of private equity in the development of affordable housing aimed at low-income Americans. The credits are also commonly called Section 42 credits in reference to the applicable section of the Internal Revenue Code. The tax credits are more attractive than tax deductions as they provide a dollar-for-dollar reduction in a taxpayer's federal income tax, whereas a tax deduction only provides a reduction in taxable income.

a. Low income housing tax credit
b. Rent control
c. 100-year flood
d. Tenant rights

20. The term _____ describes two different concepts:

- The first is a recognition of partial payment already made towards taxes due.
- The second is a state benefit paid to workers through the tax system, which has the effect of increasing (rather than reducing) net income.

Within the Australian, Canadian, United Kingdom, and United States tax systems, a _____ is a recognition of partial payment already made towards taxes due. A similar concept exists (fr:Avoir fiscal) in the French tax system. This situation arises, for example, when standard rate tax has been deducted at source , but the tax-payer is subject to further taxation at a higher rate. It also applies in dividend imputation systems.

a. 100-year flood
b. 1921 recession
c. 130-30 fund
d. Tax credit

21. To tax is to impose a financial charge or other levy upon a taxpayer by a state or the functional equivalent of a state.

_____ are also imposed by many subnational entities. _____ consist of direct tax or indirect tax, and may be paid in money or as its labour equivalent (often but not always unpaid.)

a. 100-year flood
b. 130-30 fund
c. 1921 recession
d. Taxes

22. A _____ is a bond which is worth a certain monetary value and which may only be spent for specific reasons or on specific goods. Examples include -- but are not limited to -- housing, travel and food _____s. The term _____ is also a synonym for receipt, and is often used to refer to receipts used as evidence of, for example, the declaration that a service has been performed or that an expenditure has been made.

a. 130-30 fund
b. 100-year flood
c. 1921 recession
d. Voucher

23. In a federal system of government, a _____ is a large sum of money granted by the national government to a regional government with only general provisions as to the way it is to be spent. This can be contrasted with a categorical grant which has more strict and specific provisions on the way it is to be spent.

An advantage of _____s is that they allow regional governments to experiment with different ways of spending money with the same goal in mind, though it is very difficult to compare the results of such spending and reach a conclusion.

a. Financial Industry Regulatory Authority
b. Transactions deposit
c. 100-year flood
d. Block Grant

24. _____ is a program of land re-development in areas of moderate to high density urban land use. Its modern incarnation began in the late 19th century in developed nations and experienced an intense phase in the late 1940s - under the rubric of reconstruction. The process has had a major impact on many urban landscapes, and has played an important role in the history and demographics of cities around the world, including: Beijing, China, Melbourne, Victoria; Saint John, New Brunswick; Glasgow, Scotland; Boston, Massachusetts; Warsaw; San Francisco, California; Bilbao, Spain, Canary Wharf, in London, and Cardiff Bay in Cardiff.
a. Urban renewal
b. Urban prairie
c. ACCRA Cost of Living Index
d. Urbanization

25. _____, compulsory purchase (United Kingdom, New Zealand, Ireland), resumption/compulsory acquisition (Australia) or expropriation (South Africa and Canada) or land acqusition (India) in common law legal systems is the inherent power of the state to seize a citizen's private property, expropriate property but without the owner's consent. The property is taken either for government use or by delegation to third parties who will devote it to public or civic use or, in some cases, economic development. The most common uses of property taken by _____ are for public utilities, highways, and railroads.

a. ACEA agreement
b. AD-IA Model
c. ACCRA Cost of Living Index
d. Eminent domain

26. A _____ is a place of residence or refuge and comfort. It is usually a place in which an individual or a family can rest and be able to store personal property. Most modern-day households contain sanitary facilities and a means of preparing food.
   a. 100-year flood
   b. HOME
   c. 1921 recession
   d. 130-30 fund

27. _____ is a fee paid on borrowed assets. It is the price paid for the use of borrowed money , or, money earned by deposited funds . Assets that are sometimes lent with _____ include money, shares, consumer goods through hire purchase, major assets such as aircraft, and even entire factories in finance lease arrangements.
   a. Internal debt
   b. Insolvency
   c. Asset protection
   d. Interest

28. _____ is a term used to described a tendency or preference towards a particular perspective, ideology or result, especially when the tendency interferes with the ability to be impartial, unprejudiced, or objective. The term _____ed is used to describe an action, judgment, or other outcome influenced by a prejudged perspective. It is also used to refer to a person or body of people whose actions or judgments exhibit _____.
   a. Bias
   b. 1921 recession
   c. 100-year flood
   d. 130-30 fund

29. _____ refers to laws or ordinances that set price controls on the renting of residential housing. It functions as a price ceiling.

_____ exists in approximately 40 countries around the world.

a. Tenant rights
b. National Housing Conference
c. 100-year flood
d. Rent control

30. In the study of human settlements, an _____ is an extended city or town area comprising the built-up area of a central place (usually a municipality) and any suburbs linked by continuous urban area. In France, INSEE the French Statistical Institute, translate it as 'Unité urbaine' which means continuous urbanized area. However, because of differences in definitions of what does and does not constitute an '_____', as well as variations and limitations in statistical or geographical methodology, it can be problematic to compare different _____s around the world.
    a. ACCRA Cost of Living Index
    b. ACEA agreement
    c. AD-IA Model
    d. Agglomeration

Chapter 15. The Role of Local Government

1. A _____ is the procedure of systematically acquiring and recording information about the members of a given population. It is a regularly occurring and official count of a particular population. The term is used mostly in connection with national 'population and door to door _____ es' (to be taken every 10 years according to United Nations recommendations), agriculture, and business _____ es.
   a. 1921 recession
   b. Census
   c. 100-year flood
   d. 130-30 fund

2. In economics, _____ is the transfer of income, wealth or property from some individuals to others.

One premise of _____ is that money should be distributed to benefit the poorer members of society, and that the rich have an obligation to assist the poor, thus creating a more financially egalitarian society. Another argument is that the rich exploit the poor or otherwise gain unfair benefits.

   a. 1921 recession
   b. Redistribution
   c. 100-year flood
   d. 130-30 fund

3. _____ is used to assign the available resources in an economic way. It is part of resource management.

In strategic planning, is a plan for using available resources, for example human resources, especially in the near term, to achieve goals for the future.

   a. 1921 recession
   b. Resource allocation
   c. 100-year flood
   d. 130-30 fund

4. A _____ is a broad coalition government consisting of all parties (or all major parties) in the legislature, usually formed during a time of war or other national emergency.

During World War I the Conservative government of Sir Robert Borden invited the Liberal opposition to join the government as a means of dealing with the Conscription crisis of 1917. The Liberals, led by Sir Wilfrid Laurier refused; however, Borden was able to convince many individual Liberals to join what was called a Union Government, which defeated the Laurier Liberals in the fall 1917 election.

Chapter 15. The Role of Local Government 105

a. 130-30 fund
b. 1921 recession
c. National government
d. 100-year flood

5. _____ has several particular meanings:

- in mathematics
    - _____ function
    - Euler _____
    - _____
    - _____ subgroup
    - method of _____s (partial differential equations)
- in physics and engineering
    - any _____ curve that shows the relationship between certain input- and output parameters, e.g.
    - an I-V or current-voltage _____ is the current in a circuit as a function of the applied voltage
    - Receiver-Operator _____
- in fiction
    - in Dungeons ' Dragons, _____ is another name for ability score

a. Russian financial crisis
b. Technocracy
c. Characteristic
d. Demand

6. A _____ is an object whose consumption increases the utility of the consumer, for which the quantity demanded exceeds the quantity supplied at zero price. _____s are usually modeled as having diminishing marginal utility. The first individual purchase has high utility; the second has less.
a. Merit good
b. Pie method
c. Composite good
d. Good

7. In economics, a _____ is a good that is non-rivaled and non-excludable. This means, respectively, that consumption of the good by one individual does not reduce availability of the good for consumption by others; and that no one can be effectively excluded from using the good. In the real world, there may be no such thing as an absolutely non-rivaled and non-excludable good; but economists think that some goods approximate the concept closely enough for the analysis to be economically useful.

a. Demand-pull theory
b. Public good
c. Happiness economics
d. Neoclassical synthesis

8. The _____ Tiebout migration is a public choice theory model first described by economist Charles Tiebout in his article 'A Pure Theory of Local Expenditures' The essence of the model is that there is in fact a non-political solution to the free rider problem in local governance.

Tiebout first proposed the model informally as a graduate student in a seminar with Richard Musgrave, who argued that the free rider problem necessarily required a political solution.

a. 1921 recession
b. 100-year flood
c. Tiebout model
d. 130-30 fund

9. A _____ is:

- Rewrite _____, in generative grammar and computer science
- Standardization, a formal and widely-accepted statement, fact, definition, or qualification
- Operation, a determinate _____ for performing a mathematical operation and obtaining a certain result (Mathematics, Logic)
    - Unary operation
    - Binary operation
- _____ of inference, a function from sets of formulae to formulae (Mathematics, Logic)
- _____ of thumb, principle with broad application that is not intended to be strictly accurate or reliable for every situation. Also often simply referred to as a _____
- Moral, an atomic element of a moral code for guiding choices in human behavior
- Heuristic, a quantized '_____' which shows a tendency or probability for successful function
- A regulation, as in sports
- A Production _____, as in computer science
- Procedural law, a _____ set governing the application of laws to cases
    - A law, which may informally be called a '_____'
    - A court ruling, a decision by a court
- In the U.S. Government, a regulation mandated by Congress, but written or expanded upon by the Executive Branch.
- Norm (sociology), an informal but widely accepted _____, concept, truth, definition, or qualification (social norms, legal norms, coding norms)
- Norm (philosophy), a kind of sentence or a reason to act, feel or believe
- 'Rulership' is the concept of governance by a government:
    - Military _____, governance by a military body
    - Monastic _____, a collection of precepts that guides the life of monks or nuns in a religious order where the superior holds the place of Christ
- Slide _____

- '_____,' a song by Ayumi Hamasaki
- '_____,' a song by rapper Nas
- '_____s,' an album by the band The Whitest Boy Alive
- _____s: Pyaar Ka Superhit Formula, a 2003 Bollywood film
- ruler, an instrument for measuring lengths
- _____, a component of an astrolabe, circumferator or similar instrument
- The _____s, a bestselling self-help book
- _____ Project (Run Up-to-date Linux Everywhere), a project that aims to use up-to-date Linux software on old PCs
- _____ engine, a software system that helps managing business _____s
- Ja _____, a hip hop artist
    - R.U.L.E., a 2005 greatest hits album by rapper Ja _____
- '_____s,' a KMFDM song

a. Rule
b. Technocracy
c. Demand
d. Procter ' Gamble

10. _____ is an ad valorem tax that an owner is required to pay on the value of the property being taxed. _____ can be defined as 'generally, tax imposed by municipalities upon owners of property within their jurisdiction based on the value of such property.' There are three species or types of property: Land, Improvements to Land (immovable manmade objects; i.e., buildings), and Personal (movable manmade objects.) Real estate, real property or realty are all terms for the combination of land and improvements.
   a. Bank regulation
   b. Chief Financial Officers Act of 1990
   c. Property tax
   d. Community property

11. Economics:

   - _____,the desire to own something and the ability to pay for it
   - _____ curve,a graphic representation of a _____ schedule
   - _____ deposit, the money in checking accounts
   - _____ pull theory,the theory that inflation occurs when _____ for goods and services exceeds existing supplies
   - _____ schedule,a table that lists the quantity of a good a person will buy it each different price
   - _____ side economics,the school of economics at believes government spending and tax cuts open economy by raising _____

   a. Variability
   b. Production
   c. McKesson ' Robbins scandal
   d. Demand

12. To _____ is to impose a financial charge or other levy upon a taxpayer by a state or the functional equivalent of a state.

   _____es are also imposed by many subnational entities. _____es consist of direct _____ or indirect _____, and may be paid in money or as its labour equivalent (often but not always unpaid.)

Chapter 15. The Role of Local Government

a. Tax
b. 130-30 fund
c. 100-year flood
d. 1921 recession

13. To tax is to impose a financial charge or other levy upon a taxpayer by a state or the functional equivalent of a state. _____ are also imposed by many subnational entities. _____ consist of direct tax or indirect tax, and may be paid in money or as its labour equivalent (often but not always unpaid.)

a. 130-30 fund
b. 100-year flood
c. 1921 recession
d. Taxes

14. In calculus, a function f defined on a subset of the real numbers with real values is called _____, if for all x and y such that x >≤ y one has f(x) >≤ f(y), so f preserves the order. In layman's terms, the sign of the slope is always positive (the curve tending upwards) or zero (i.e., non-decreasing, or asymptotic, or depicted as a horizontal, flat line) Likewise, a function is called monotonically decreasing (non-increasing) if, whenever x >≤ y, then f(x) >≥ f(y), so it reverses the order.

a. 130-30 fund
b. 100-year flood
c. 1921 recession
d. Monotonic

15. In economics, a _____ occurs when, due to the economies of scale of a particular industry, the maximum efficiency of production and distribution is realized through a single supplier.

Natural monopolies arise where the largest supplier in an industry, often the first supplier in a market, has an overwhelming cost advantage over other actual or potential competitors. This tends to be the case in industries where capital costs predominate, creating economies of scale which are large in relation to the size of the market, and hence high barriers to entry; examples include water services and electricity.

a. Common-pool resource
b. Collective goods
c. Natural monopoly
d. Privatizing profits and socializing losses

16. In economics, a _____ exists when a specific individual or enterprise has sufficient control over a particular product or service to determine significantly the terms on which other individuals shall have access to it. Monopolies are thus characterized by a lack of economic competition for the good or service that they provide and a lack of viable substitute goods. The verb 'monopolize' refers to the process by which a firm gains persistently greater market share than what is expected under perfect competition.
   a. 130-30 fund
   b. 100-year flood
   c. Monopoly
   d. 1921 recession

17. In economics, _____ and economies of scale are related terms that describe what happens as the scale of production increases. They are different terms and should not be used interchangeably.

   _____ refers to a technical property of production that examines changes in output subsequent to a proportional change in all inputs (where all inputs increase by a constant factor.)

   a. Returns to scale
   b. Constant returns to scale
   c. Customer equity
   d. Necessity good

18. _____ refers to the stock of skills and knowledge embodied in the ability to perform labor so as to produce economic value. It is the skills and knowledge gained by a worker through education and experience. Many early economic theories refer to it simply as labor, one of three factors of production, and consider it to be a fungible resource -- homogeneous and easily interchangeable. Other conceptions of labor dispense with these assumptions.
   a. Law of increasing costs
   b. Human capital
   c. General equilibrium
   d. Price theory

19. _____ is the shortage of common things such as food, clothing, shelter and safe drinking water, all of which determine the quality of life. It may also include the lack of access to opportunities such as education and employment which aid the escape from _____ and/or allow one to enjoy the respect of fellow citizens. According to Mollie Orshansky who developed the _____ measurements used by the U.S. government, 'to be poor is to be deprived of those goods and services and pleasures which others around us take for granted.' Ongoing debates over causes, effects and best ways to measure _____, directly influence the design and implementation of _____-reduction programs and are therefore relevant to the fields of public administration and international development.

a. Growth Elasticity of Poverty
b. Liberal welfare reforms
c. Poverty map
d. Poverty

20. _____ is the incidence or process of transferring ownership of a business, enterprise, agency or public service from the public sector (government) to the private sector (business.) In a broader sense, _____ refers to transfer of any government function to the private sector including governmental functions like revenue collection and law enforcement.

The term '_____' also has been used to describe two unrelated transactions.

a. Performance reports
b. Ricardian equivalence
c. Compound empowerment
d. Privatization

21. _____ is a form of housing tenure in which the property is owned by a government authority, which may be central or local. Social housing is an umbrella term referring to rental housing which may be owned and managed by the state, by not-for-profit organizations, or by a combination of the two, usually with the aim of providing affordable housing.

Although the common goal of _____ is to provide affordable housing, the details, terminology, definitions of poverty and other criteria for allocation vary.

a. Public housing
b. 1921 recession
c. 100-year flood
d. 130-30 fund

22. A _____ is a bond which is worth a certain monetary value and which may only be spent for specific reasons or on specific goods. Examples include -- but are not limited to -- housing, travel and food _____s. The term _____ is also a synonym for receipt, and is often used to refer to receipts used as evidence of, for example, the declaration that a service has been performed or that an expenditure has been made.
a. 130-30 fund
b. 100-year flood
c. 1921 recession
d. Voucher

Chapter 15. The Role of Local Government

23. The _____ is 'the basic residential unit in which economic production, consumption, inheritance, child rearing, and shelter are organized and carried out'; [the _____] 'may or may not be synonomous with family'.

The _____ is the basic unit of analysis in many social, microeconomic and government models. The term refers to all individuals who live in the same dwelling.

   a. Family economics
   b. 100-year flood
   c. 130-30 fund
   d. Household

24. In the study of human settlements, an _____ is an extended city or town area comprising the built-up area of a central place (usually a municipality) and any suburbs linked by continuous urban area. In France, INSEE the French Statistical Institute, translate it as 'Unité urbaine' which means continuous urbanized area. However, because of differences in definitions of what does and does not constitute an '_____', as well as variations and limitations in statistical or geographical methodology, it can be problematic to compare different _____s around the world.
   a. AD-IA Model
   b. ACEA agreement
   c. ACCRA Cost of Living Index
   d. Agglomeration

25. _____, in microeconomics, are the cost advantages that a business obtains due to expansion. They are factors that cause a producere;s average cost per unit to fall as scale is increased. _____ is a long run concept and refers to reductions in unit cost as the size of a facility, or scale, increases.
   a. Underinvestment employment relationship
   b. Isoquant
   c. Economic production quantity
   d. Economies of scale

26. A municipality is an administrative entity composed of a clearly defined territory and its population and commonly denotes a city, town or a small grouping of them. A municipality is typically governed by a mayor and a city council or _____ council.

The notion of municipality includes townships but is not restricted to them.

a. 1921 recession
b. 100-year flood
c. Municipal
d. 130-30 fund

27. _____ in economics and business is the result of an exchange and from that trade we assign a numerical monetary value to a good, service or asset. If Alice trades Bob 4 apples for an orange, the _____ of an orange is 4 apples. Inversely, the _____ of an apple is 1/4 oranges.
a. Price
b. Price war
c. Premium pricing
d. Price book

Chapter 16. Local Government Revenue

1. In a federal system of government, a _____ is a large sum of money granted by the national government to a regional government with only general provisions as to the way it is to be spent. This can be contrasted with a categorical grant which has more strict and specific provisions on the way it is to be spent.

An advantage of _____s is that they allow regional governments to experiment with different ways of spending money with the same goal in mind, though it is very difficult to compare the results of such spending and reach a conclusion.

   a. 100-year flood
   b. Financial Industry Regulatory Authority
   c. Transactions deposit
   d. Block Grant

2. _____ is an ad valorem tax that an owner is required to pay on the value of the property being taxed. _____ can be defined as 'generally, tax imposed by municipalities upon owners of property within their jurisdiction based on the value of such property.' There are three species or types of property: Land, Improvements to Land (immovable manmade objects; i.e., buildings), and Personal (movable manmade objects.) Real estate, real property or realty are all terms for the combination of land and improvements.
   a. Property tax
   b. Community property
   c. Chief Financial Officers Act of 1990
   d. Bank regulation

3. The _____ Tiebout migration is a public choice theory model first described by economist Charles Tiebout in his article 'A Pure Theory of Local Expenditures' The essence of the model is that there is in fact a non-political solution to the free rider problem in local governance.

Tiebout first proposed the model informally as a graduate student in a seminar with Richard Musgrave, who argued that the free rider problem necessarily required a political solution.

   a. 1921 recession
   b. 100-year flood
   c. Tiebout model
   d. 130-30 fund

4. A _____ is the transfer of wealth from one party (such as a person or company) to another. A _____ is usually made in exchange for the provision of goods, services or both, or to fulfill a legal obligation.

The simplest and oldest form of _____ is barter, the exchange of one good or service for another.

a. Going concern
b. Soft count
c. Payment
d. Social gravity

5. A _____ is:

- Rewrite _____, in generative grammar and computer science
- Standardization, a formal and widely-accepted statement, fact, definition, or qualification
- Operation, a determinate _____ for performing a mathematical operation and obtaining a certain result (Mathematics, Logic)
    - Unary operation
    - Binary operation
- _____ of inference, a function from sets of formulae to formulae (Mathematics, Logic)
- _____ of thumb, principle with broad application that is not intended to be strictly accurate or reliable for every situation. Also often simply referred to as a _____
- Moral, an atomic element of a moral code for guiding choices in human behavior
- Heuristic, a quantized '_____' which shows a tendency or probability for successful function
- A regulation, as in sports
- A Production _____, as in computer science
- Procedural law, a _____ set governing the application of laws to cases
    - A law, which may informally be called a '_____'
    - A court ruling, a decision by a court
- In the U.S. Government, a regulation mandated by Congress, but written or expanded upon by the Executive Branch.
- Norm (sociology), an informal but widely accepted _____, concept, truth, definition, or qualification (social norms, legal norms, coding norms)
- Norm (philosophy), a kind of sentence or a reason to act, feel or believe
- 'Rulership' is the concept of governance by a government:
    - Military _____, governance by a military body
    - Monastic _____, a collection of precepts that guides the life of monks or nuns in a religious order where the superior holds the place of Christ
- Slide _____

- '_____,' a song by Ayumi Hamasaki
- '_____,' a song by rapper Nas
- '_____s,' an album by the band The Whitest Boy Alive
- _____s: Pyaar Ka Superhit Formula, a 2003 Bollywood film
- ruler, an instrument for measuring lengths
- _____, a component of an astrolabe, circumferator or similar instrument
- The _____s, a bestselling self-help book
- _____ Project (Run Up-to-date Linux Everywhere), a project that aims to use up-to-date Linux software on old PCs
- _____ engine, a software system that helps managing business _____s
- Ja _____, a hip hop artist
    - R.U.L.E., a 2005 greatest hits album by rapper Ja _____
- '_____s,' a KMFDM song

a. Rule
b. Technocracy
c. Procter ' Gamble
d. Demand

6. To _____ is to impose a financial charge or other levy upon a taxpayer by a state or the functional equivalent of a state.

_____es are also imposed by many subnational entities. _____es consist of direct _____ or indirect _____, and may be paid in money or as its labour equivalent (often but not always unpaid.)

a. 100-year flood
b. 130-30 fund
c. 1921 recession
d. Tax

7. To tax is to impose a financial charge or other levy upon a taxpayer by a state or the functional equivalent of a state.

_____ are also imposed by many subnational entities. _____ consist of direct tax or indirect tax, and may be paid in money or as its labour equivalent (often but not always unpaid.)

a. 130-30 fund
b. 100-year flood
c. 1921 recession
d. Taxes

8. A _____ is the procedure of systematically acquiring and recording information about the members of a given population. It is a regularly occurring and official count of a particular population. The term is used mostly in connection with national 'population and door to door _____es' (to be taken every 10 years according to United Nations recommendations), agriculture, and business _____es.
a. 100-year flood
b. 1921 recession
c. 130-30 fund
d. Census

9. _____ is a mechanism that allows people easily to buy and sell products. Services are often included in the scope of the term. _____ regulation is an economic term that describes restrictions in the market.

a. Fixed exchange rate system
b. Financialization
c. Product market
d. Market dominance

10. A _____ is a type of economic equilibrium, where the clearance on the market of some specific goods is obtained independently from prices and quantities demanded and supplied in other markets. In other words, the prices of all substitutes and complements, as well as income levels of consumers are constant. Here the dynamic process is that prices adjust until supply equals demand.
   a. Market system
   b. Market depth
   c. Horizontal market
   d. Partial equilibrium

11. _____ is a form of housing tenure in which the property is owned by a government authority, which may be central or local. Social housing is an umbrella term referring to rental housing which may be owned and managed by the state, by not-for-profit organizations, or by a combination of the two, usually with the aim of providing affordable housing.

Although the common goal of _____ is to provide affordable housing, the details, terminology, definitions of poverty and other criteria for allocation vary.

   a. 100-year flood
   b. Public housing
   c. 1921 recession
   d. 130-30 fund

12. _____ is a fee paid on borrowed assets. It is the price paid for the use of borrowed money, or, money earned by deposited funds. Assets that are sometimes lent with _____ include money, shares, consumer goods through hire purchase, major assets such as aircraft, and even entire factories in finance lease arrangements.
   a. Insolvency
   b. Asset protection
   c. Interest
   d. Internal debt

Chapter 16. Local Government Revenue

13. In the study of human settlements, an _____ is an extended city or town area comprising the built-up area of a central place (usually a municipality) and any suburbs linked by continuous urban area. In France, INSEE the French Statistical Institute, translate it as 'Unité urbaine' which means continuous urbanized area. However, because of differences in definitions of what does and does not constitute an '_____', as well as variations and limitations in statistical or geographical methodology, it can be problematic to compare different _____s around the world.
    a. ACEA agreement
    b. ACCRA Cost of Living Index
    c. Agglomeration
    d. AD-IA Model

14. _____s are a type of administrative division, in some countries managed by a local government. They vary greatly in size, spanning entire regions or counties, several municipalities, or subdivisions of municipalities.

In Austria, a _____ or Bezirk is an administrative division normally encompassing several municipalities, roughly equivalent to the Landkreis in Germany.

    a. District
    b. 130-30 fund
    c. 1921 recession
    d. 100-year flood

15. _____ occurs when a country (or other jurisdiction) encourages economic activity to move to another country (or jurisdiction) because its taxes are too high. This is more likely if the economic activity is more mobile. For example, land is not mobile, so it is difficult (if not impossible) for a country to export land taxes to another country.
    a. Nil-rate band
    b. Franchise tax
    c. Current use
    d. Tax exporting

16. A _____ is an object whose consumption increases the utility of the consumer, for which the quantity demanded exceeds the quantity supplied at zero price. _____s are usually modeled as having diminishing marginal utility. The first individual purchase has high utility; the second has less.
    a. Merit good
    b. Composite good
    c. Good
    d. Pie method

17. In economics, a _____ is a good that is non-rivaled and non-excludable. This means, respectively, that consumption of the good by one individual does not reduce availability of the good for consumption by others; and that no one can be effectively excluded from using the good. In the real world, there may be no such thing as an absolutely non-rivaled and non-excludable good; but economists think that some goods approximate the concept closely enough for the analysis to be economically useful.

   a. Demand-pull theory
   b. Happiness economics
   c. Neoclassical synthesis
   d. Public good

18. The _____ was a worldwide economic downturn starting in most places in 1929 and ending at different times in the 1930s or early 1940s for different countries. It was the largest and most important economic depression in the 20th century, and is used in the 21st century as an example of how far the world's economy can fall. The _____ originated in the United States; historians most often use as a starting date the stock market crash on October 29, 1929, known as Black Tuesday.

   a. Jarrow March
   b. Wall Street Crash of 1929
   c. British Empire Economic Conference
   d. Great Depression

19. A _____ is a reduction in taxes. Economic stimulus via _____s, along with interest rate intervention and deficit spending, are one of the central tenets of Keynesian economics.

The immediate effects of a _____ are, generally, a decrease in the real income of the government and an increase in the real income of those whose tax rate has been lowered.

   a. Withholding tax
   b. Popiwek
   c. Tax cut
   d. Direct taxes

20. _____ is a broad label that refers to any individuals or households that use goods and services generated within the economy. The concept of a _____ is used in different contexts, so that the usage and significance of the term may vary.

Typically when business people and economists talk of _____s they are talking about person as _____, an aggregated commodity item with little individuality other than that expressed in the buy/not-buy decision.

a. Consumer
b. 1921 recession
c. 100-year flood
d. 130-30 fund

21. _____ is the shortage of common things such as food, clothing, shelter and safe drinking water, all of which determine the quality of life. It may also include the lack of access to opportunities such as education and employment which aid the escape from _____ and/or allow one to enjoy the respect of fellow citizens. According to Mollie Orshansky who developed the _____ measurements used by the U.S. government, 'to be poor is to be deprived of those goods and services and pleasures which others around us take for granted.' Ongoing debates over causes, effects and best ways to measure _____, directly influence the design and implementation of _____-reduction programs and are therefore relevant to the fields of public administration and international development.

a. Growth Elasticity of Poverty
b. Poverty map
c. Liberal welfare reforms
d. Poverty

22. The _____ is 'the basic residential unit in which economic production, consumption, inheritance, child rearing, and shelter are organized and carried out'; [the _____] 'may or may not be synonymous with family'.

The _____ is the basic unit of analysis in many social, microeconomic and government models. The term refers to all individuals who live in the same dwelling.

a. Family economics
b. 100-year flood
c. 130-30 fund
d. Household

23. _____ refers to the stock of skills and knowledge embodied in the ability to perform labor so as to produce economic value. It is the skills and knowledge gained by a worker through education and experience. Many early economic theories refer to it simply as labor, one of three factors of production, and consider it to be a fungible resource -- homogeneous and easily interchangeable. Other conceptions of labor dispense with these assumptions.

a. Law of increasing costs
b. Price theory
c. General equilibrium
d. Human capital

24. A _____ is a scenario 'in which a poor country is simply too poor to achieve sustained economic growth.' The trap becomes cyclical and begins to reinforce itself if steps are not taken to break the cycle. Depending upon a persone;s origin of birth, they may find themselves financially stable their entire lives, or at the other extreme, they may find themselves born into severe poverty that seems utterly inescapable. Many factors contribute to a _____, and these factors vary from case to case.
   a. Adolph Fischer
   b. Adolf Hitler
   c. Adam Smith
   d. Poverty trap

25. _____ in economics and business is the result of an exchange and from that trade we assign a numerical monetary value to a good, service or asset. If Alice trades Bob 4 apples for an orange, the _____ of an orange is 4 apples. Inversely, the _____ of an apple is 1/4 oranges.
   a. Price book
   b. Price
   c. Premium pricing
   d. Price war

26. _____ is the term denoting either an entrance or changes which are inserted into a system and which activate/modify a process. It is an abstract concept, used in the modeling, system(s) design and system(s) exploitation. It is usually connected with other terms, e.g., _____ field, _____ variable, _____ parameter, _____ value, _____ signal, _____ device and _____ file.
   a. AD-IA Model
   b. ACEA agreement
   c. ACCRA Cost of Living Index
   d. Input

27. _____ is a branch of economics that studies how individuals, households and firms and some states make decisions to allocate limited resources, typically in markets where goods or services are being bought and sold. _____ examines how these decisions and behaviours affect the supply and demand for goods and services, which determines prices; and how prices, in turn , determine the supply and demand of goods and services.

Whereas macroeconomics involves the 'sum total of economic activity, dealing with the issues of growth, inflation and unemployment, and with national economic policies relating to these issues' and the effects of government actions on them.

a. Recession
b. Countercyclical
c. New Keynesian economics
d. Microeconomics

28. _____ in economics refers to metrics and measures of output from production processes, per unit of input. Labor _____, for example, is typically measured as a ratio of output per labor-hour, an input. _____ may be conceived of as a metrics of the technical or engineering efficiency of production.
   a. Productivity
   b. Fordism
   c. Piece work
   d. Production-possibility frontier

29. Economics:

   - _____,the desire to own something and the ability to pay for it
   - _____ curve,a graphic representation of a _____ schedule
   - _____ deposit, the money in checking accounts
   - _____ pull theory,the theory that inflation occurs when _____ for goods and services exceeds existing supplies
   - _____ schedule,a table that lists the quantity of a good a person will buy it each different price
   - _____ side economics,the school of economics at believes government spending and tax cuts open economy by raising _____

   a. Production
   b. McKesson ' Robbins scandal
   c. Variability
   d. Demand

30. In economics, the _____ is the change in consumption resulting from a change in real income.

Another important item that can change is the money income of the consumer. The _____ is the phenomenon observed through changes in purchasing power.

a. Income effect
b. Equilibrium wage
c. Inflation hedge
d. Export subsidy

31. In microeconomics, _____ is quite simply the conversion of inputs into outputs. It is an economic process that uses resources to create a good or service that is suitable for exchange. This can include manufacturing, storing, shipping, and packaging.
    a. MET
    b. Red Guards
    c. Solved
    d. Production

32. The term surplus is used in economics for several related quantities. The _____ is the amount that consumers benefit by being able to purchase a product for a price that is less than they would be willing to pay. The producer surplus is the amount that producers benefit by selling at a market price mechanism that is higher than they would be willing to sell for.
    a. Microeconomic reform
    b. Necessity good
    c. Marginal rate of technical substitution
    d. Consumer surplus

33. The term surplus is used in economics for several related quantities. The consumer surplus is the amount that consumers benefit by being able to purchase a product for a price that is less than they would be willing to pay. The _____ is the amount that producers benefit by selling at a market price mechanism that is higher than they would be willing to sell for.
    a. Long term
    b. Schedule delay
    c. Returns to scale
    d. Producer surplus

34. The _____ is the number of total hours that workers wish to work at a given real wage rate.

Labor supply curves are derived from the 'labor-leisure' trade-off. More hours worked earn higher incomes but necessitate a cut in the amount of leisure that workers enjoy.

a. De minimis fringe benefits
b. Dual labor market
c. Compound interest
d. Supply of labor

35. In microeconomic theory, an _____ is a graph showing different bundles of goods, each measured as to quantity, between which a consumer is indifferent. That is, at each point on the curve, the consumer has no preference for one bundle over another. In other words, they are all equally preferred.
   a. Engel curve
   b. Indifference curve
   c. Indifference map
   d. Expenditure minimization problem

36. In economics, the _____ is the rate at which a consumer is ready to give up one good in exchange for another good while maintaining the same level of satisfaction.

Under the standard assumption of neoclassical economics that goods and services are continuously divisible, the marginal rates of substitution will be the same regardless of the direction of exchange, and will correspond to the slope of an indifference curve (more precisely, to the slope multiplied by -1) passing through the consumption bundle in question, at that point: mathematically, it is the implicit derivative. MRS of Y for X is the amount of Y for which a consumer is willing to exchange for X locally.

   a. Demand vacuum
   b. Marginal rate of substitution
   c. Quality bias
   d. Supply and demand

37. In economics, an _____ is a contour line drawn through the set of points at which the same quantity of output is produced while changing the quantities of two or more inputs. While an indifference curve helps to answer the utility-maximizing problem of consumers, the _____ deals with the cost-minimization problem of producers. _____s are typically drawn on capital-labor graphs, showing the tradeoff between capital and labor in the production function, and the decreasing marginal returns of both inputs.
   a. Economic production quantity
   b. Economies of scale
   c. Underinvestment employment relationship
   d. Isoquant

38. In economics, the _____ or the Technical Rate of Substitution (TRS) is the amount by which the quantity of one input has to be reduced ($-\Delta x_2$) when one extra unit of another input is used ($\Delta x_1 = 1$), so that output remains constant ($y = \bar{y}$.)

$$MRTS(x_1, x_2) = \frac{\Delta x_2}{\Delta x_1} = -\frac{MP_1}{MP_2}$$

where MP_1 and MP_2 are the marginal products of input 1 and input 2, respectively.

Along an isoquant, the MRTS shows the rate at which one input (e.g. capital or labor) may be substituted for another, while maintaining the same level of output.

a. Household production function
b. Pork cycle
c. Producer surplus
d. Marginal rate of technical substitution

39. In economics an _____ line represents a combination of inputs which all cost the same amount. Although similar to the budget constraint in consumer theory, the use of the _____ pertains to cost-minimization in production, as opposed to utility-maximization. The typical _____ line represents the ratio of costs of labour and capital, so the formula is often written as:

$$rK + wL = C$$

Where w represents the wage of labour, and r represents the rental rate of capital.

a. Incentive
b. Isocost
c. Inventory analysis
d. Epstein-Zin preferences

40. A _____ is an expression that compares quantities relative to each other. The most common examples involve two quantities, but any number of quantities can be compared. _____s are represented mathematically by separating each quantity with a colon, for example the _____ 2:3, which is read as the _____ 'two to three'.

a. Y-intercept
b. Ratio
c. 130-30 fund
d. 100-year flood

ANSWER KEY

Chapter 1
1. a   2. d   3. a   4. d   5. d   6. a   7. d   8. c   9. c   10. c
11. b   12. d   13. a   14. b   15. d   16. a   17. b   18. a   19. a

Chapter 2
1. a   2. d   3. b   4. d   5. d   6. d   7. d   8. d   9. b   10. a
11. b   12. d   13. a   14. d   15. a   16. a   17. d   18. b   19. c   20. b
21. d   22. a   23. c   24. b   25. a

Chapter 3
1. d   2. d   3. a   4. b   5. c   6. b   7. d   8. d   9. d   10. b
11. d   12. a   13. a   14. b   15. a

Chapter 4
1. d   2. b   3. a   4. d   5. b   6. d   7. d   8. d   9. d

Chapter 5
1. d   2. d   3. a   4. d   5. c   6. c   7. a   8. d   9. b   10. c
11. d   12. b   13. d   14. a   15. a   16. d   17. d   18. b   19. b   20. b
21. d   22. a   23. b   24. c   25. d   26. d   27. c   28. d   29. d

Chapter 6
1. d   2. d   3. d   4. d   5. d   6. d   7. d   8. a   9. a   10. c
11. c   12. d   13. d   14. a   15. c   16. b   17. d

Chapter 7
1. c   2. d   3. d   4. b   5. a   6. d   7. d   8. c   9. b   10. d
11. a   12. d   13. a   14. d   15. a   16. b   17. b   18. b   19. d   20. a
21. b   22. d   23. d   24. c   25. d   26. c   27. d   28. d   29. c   30. d
31. c   32. d   33. c   34. c   35. b   36. d

Chapter 8
1. b   2. c   3. b   4. d   5. b   6. d   7. d   8. c   9. d   10. a
11. a   12. d   13. a   14. b   15. b   16. a   17. d   18. a   19. b   20. d
21. d   22. c   23. b   24. b   25. a   26. d   27. d   28. c   29. c   30. d
31. a   32. a   33. d   34. d   35. a   36. b   37. c

Chapter 9
1. a   2. b   3. d   4. a   5. a   6. d   7. b   8. a   9. c   10. d
11. d   12. d   13. a   14. d   15. d   16. b   17. c   18. d   19. c   20. a
21. d   22. d   23. b   24. d   25. c   26. b   27. c   28. d   29. d   30. d
31. d   32. c   33. b

Chapter 10
1. d   2. d   3. d   4. a   5. a   6. b   7. d   8. d   9. d   10. a
11. a   12. c   13. a   14. b   15. d   16. d   17. d   18. d   19. b   20. b
21. b

Chapter 11
1. a   2. d   3. d   4. d   5. c   6. d   7. d   8. d   9. d   10. a
11. d   12. d   13. d   14. c   15. d   16. d   17. d   18. d   19. d   20. d
21. d   22. d   23. a   24. b   25. d

Chapter 12
1. a   2. b   3. d   4. d   5. d   6. d   7. d   8. c   9. b   10. a
11. d

Chapter 13
1. c   2. d   3. b   4. d   5. c   6. a   7. d   8. a   9. c   10. d
11. c   12. a   13. d

Chapter 14
1. c   2. d   3. d   4. d   5. b   6. d   7. a   8. d   9. d   10. d
11. c   12. d   13. d   14. b   15. c   16. d   17. d   18. c   19. a   20. d
21. d   22. d   23. d   24. a   25. d   26. b   27. d   28. a   29. d   30. d

Chapter 15
1. b   2. b   3. b   4. c   5. c   6. d   7. b   8. c   9. a   10. c
11. d   12. a   13. d   14. d   15. c   16. c   17. a   18. b   19. d   20. d
21. a   22. d   23. d   24. d   25. d   26. c   27. a

Chapter 16
1. d   2. a   3. c   4. c   5. a   6. d   7. d   8. d   9. c   10. d
11. b   12. c   13. c   14. a   15. d   16. c   17. d   18. d   19. c   20. a
21. d   22. d   23. d   24. d   25. b   26. d   27. d   28. a   29. d   30. a
31. d   32. d   33. d   34. d   35. b   36. b   37. d   38. d   39. b   40. b

www.ingramcontent.com/pod-product-compliance
Lightning Source LLC
Chambersburg PA
CBHW082046230426

43670CB00016B/2798